UNREMEMBERED

UNREME

MBERED

TALES OF THE NEARLY FAMOUS &
THE NOT QUITE FORGOTTEN

KEN ZURSKI

AUTHOR OF *PEORIA STORIES* &
THE WRECK OF THE COLUMBIA

Unremembered: Tales of the Nearly Famous & the Not Quite Forgotten
© Copyright 2018, Ken Zurski

First Edition   ISBN 13: 978-1-937484-62-0

AMIKA PRESS   466 Central AVE #23 Northfield IL 60093   847 920 8084
info@amikapress.com   Available for purchase on amikapress.com

Edited by Jay Amberg, Mark Henry Larson and Amy Sawyer. Cover design by Sarah Koz and John Rose. Front cover photograph credits on pages 32, 63, 90, 127, 134, and 204. Cover background photography by Charles Williams. Title photograph: RMS *Mauretania,* The Library of Congress, the Bain Collection [1918]. Author photograph by Ed Emmons. Index by Stephen Seddon. Designed and typeset by Sarah Koz. Set in Walbaum, designed by Walbaum Justus Erich in 1800, digitized by František Štorm in 2010. Thanks to Nathan Matteson.

To my children, Sam and Nora,
and their curious minds.

"Swept along as I am in the current of your eventful life, I can still stop to realize that your history is simply marvelous. Every event seems to fit into the other event like the block in a child's puzzle. Does it not seem strange to you?" –*Elizabeth Custer, in a letter to her husband General George Armstrong Custer*

As with anything as subjective as the word "forgotten," the historical contributions of the people and events that fill this book can be interpreted in many ways. In this regard, there are names you may recognize and some you may not. Here, they represent, in subject and context at least, the connection and advancement of pertaining themes. To reduce the number of back notes, where possible, sources such as newspapers, magazines, books, or other periodicals are listed within the text. Any opinions or speculation by other authors are duly noted. Some quotes, either spoken or written, while not changing the substance of the thought or content, have been adapted slightly for clarity.

Contents

"Awful Conflagration of the Steam Boat *Lexington*". The Library of Congress, Popular Graphic Arts Collection, Currier and Ives [1840].

Part I

◗ Samuel Hutchinson received the awful news, as did others, on that chilly night in January 1840. A steamboat had caught fire in the Sound near Smithtown, New York, off the northern coast of Long Island. Word was spreading quickly and speculation was running rampant as to which boat that left port that night was in peril and who was on board.

Hutchinson, who lived in nearby Riverhead, was asked to help. "Be on the lookout for debris, or worse yet, bodies that might drift in with the surf," he was told. Several locals had already found a battered lifeboat washed up on shore. No one was on it, but there was a coat in her with a letter addressed to a Mr. or Captain Manchester.

Somewhere out on the Sound, a boat was indeed burning. Second Mate David Crowley was among the first to notice the flames. He organized a bucket brigade to help quell the blaze, only to find out but quickly that they were short on buckets. Then he spotted several wooden crates that were used to carry silver in coins from the Merchant Bank. Dumping the coins onto the deck, he began filling the empty crates with water. The money was of no concern now. "Save the boat and you save lives," was Crowley's thinking.

A few lifeboats were launched, but to little avail. The ship was still moving at a rapid pace, and lowering the boats safely into the water was nearly impossible. Crowley knew the end was near. Even the captain had abandoned ship. For nearly all of the passengers, jumping overboard was the only recourse and Crowley watched as they fell helplessly one by one into the frigid water. Dear God, he thought to himself, it was every man, woman, and child for themselves now.

Nearly two days later, at Samuel Hutchinson's father's house, there was an unexpected knock at the door. "A young man came to my father's in a very exhausted condition," Hutchinson described in a letter he wrote to a local newspaper. "His feet and hands were frozen stiff like marble and he was without coat or hat."

In a feeble voice, the man said he was from Providence, and that he was the second mate of the steamer *Lexington*. The boat had burned and the hull had sunk. He had managed to jump into the water and had floated ashore opposite the house, on a bale of cotton.

By now it was Wednesday. The boat had gone down late Monday night. The exhausted man had been in the water for nearly two full days and drifted at least 50 miles before finally landing against an ice pack. From there, he spotted a house nearly a mile away. He crawled across the ice and stumbled over land until he reached the front door.

Hutchinson's father, Mathias, led the hapless victim inside. Setting him near the fireplace, he cut off his boots and immersed his feet in lukewarm water. "We have taken the best care we could of him," Hutchinson continued, "but his feet are very much swollen, and what the result will be is somewhat doubtful."

The second mate's next words, however, chilled them all to the bone.

"He is of the opinion that very few passengers or crewmembers are saved," Hutchinson wrote, then concluded the letter ominously: "...or perhaps none but himself."

1

As perfect an engine as I had ever seen

⅏ On January 13, 1840, the *Lexington* steamed out of port in New York City's Upper Bay, continued up the East River around Rikers Island, and followed the north shore of the Long Island Sound bound for Stonington, Connecticut, a small coastal village where passengers destined for Boston could board a train for the remainder of the trip inland. Although by today's standards the 140-mile trip would be considered a relatively short commute, battling the rough coastline waters that acted like a speed bump to a heavy paddle wheeler still took the better part of a day. On this particular evening, however, the *Lexington,* packed with commuters, would only make it halfway.

It was a frigid night on the East Coast. By the time the boat slid from its mooring, the temperature was expected to drop several degrees below zero. Normally, despite the bitter cold, some of an estimated 144 people aboard would venture outside to the deck rails to witness the grand sight of the harbor lights fading in the distance. But this was January in New York and few took the luxury of spending even mere minutes on the outside before the bite of winter forced them back in. However, the sub-zero weather meant something else for the ship's crew: the threat of seawater ice. Captain George Child, a cautious skipper, warned his pilot that he could encounter the floating ice packs before reaching Stonington. The man at the wheel, Stephen Manchester, a captain himself, but on this night serving as the steersman, agreed.

Directly below Manchester in the pilothouse was the *Lexington*'s largest passenger by volume: 150 bales of cotton, packed so tightly that one column was supported against the casing of the smokestack. The rest of the cargo, mostly passengers' belongings, was stacked around the engine shields and tied together so they wouldn't shift even if the boat encountered heavy waves.

The winter sun had just dipped below Manhattan Island, and the shadows cast by its glow were fading. The sky was darkening and the waters were turning black with the night. The concern now for the captain was a simple one: make sure the passengers enjoyed the trip. The *Lexington* was a solidly built boat and one of the fastest on the Sound. It was also one of the most luxurious.

Luxury was no doubt the intention of its owner, Cornelius Vanderbilt, the wealthy shipping and railroad magnate. A figure certainly not lost to time, Vanderbilt was nevertheless a somewhat elusive man in private. His business dealings are mostly on record, so it's possible to establish what the man did and when he did it. But more personal detail of how he did it and why is what biographers crave. Even author T.J. Stiles, who wrote a 600-plus-page book about Vanderbilt titled *The First Tycoon,* admits his project was "a test of wills." Here's what is known: Vanderbilt made a fortune in shipping, both by land and sea. Today, many associate his name with the railroads since they eclipsed the steamboat industry in importance and historical significance, but his shrewd and effective stronghold of river traffic on the Hudson River and Long Island Sound is where he got his start.

In the mid-1800s, Vanderbilt managed several ship lines between New York and Albany, each one meant to compete with the powerful lobby of the Hudson River Steamboat Association, which monopolized the market by either buying or forcing smaller lines out of business. But Vanderbilt played his hand carefully. He continued to strengthen his own armada of ships and, by keeping fares low, threatened the Steamboat Transportation Company into extinction.

Until then, Vanderbilt resisted offers to sell, but he was a businessman first and a public advocate second. He always waited until the time was right, and in the spring of 1835, the time was right. When the frozen and choked Hudson was once again reopened to riverboat traffic, the boats owned by Vanderbilt were conspicuously missing. The public was dumbfounded. What happened to their cheap fares? In brief, their man had sold out. Vanderbilt had forced the monopoly to pay him an astronomical $100,000 to leave and another $5,000 annually to stay away. By waiting and holding a strong hand, Vanderbilt set a precedent that would continue throughout the rest of his life. He was off the Hudson for now, and on to the Sound. This time, there was more at stake.

A conglomerate of New York businessmen had organized the first of what would be three railway lines that connected passengers and freight between Boston and Rhode Island. Construction of a continuous rail line proved too costly, but a relatively short land-sea route would be more efficient. Steamboats would carry passengers between New York and the New England ports and rail cars would take them the rest of the way inland. So, Vanderbilt built the *Lexington* to compete with the other boats. The boat was necessary to carry cotton, he explained, a claim which came with some merit. Cotton, a commodity in high demand in Britain, was exported from the South to New York either by boat or rail and shipped overseas. These same ships, in return, carried goods back to the United States. New York financiers profited handsomely for the privilege to transport cotton on their boats, but not all ship owners wanted to cross the Atlantic. The water wheel mills in New England needed cotton too, and the fabrics made in these factories then came back to New York workshops to be transformed into fine clothing.

"Make her as strong as possible," Vanderbilt instructed.

The demand for more speed was a challenge. *How do you make a paddle wheeler go faster?* Vanderbilt's plan was simple, yet ingenious. The twin paddles would be built larger than most. The engine, even a single one, could be produced that nearly doubled the speed of the fastest boat of its time, the *North America,* which ran at an unprecedented 384 feet per minute or 4.3 miles per hour.

Vanderbilt wanted his boat to go double that, and the bigger paddlewheels would certainly help. Moreover, since they would take
fewer revolutions to generate more power, they would save on fuel
as well. For more efficiency, the hull was built long and narrow.
Although this posed a structural issue called "hogging," or sagging
in the middle due to weight, Vanderbilt corrected the problem by
calling for an arched deck, similar to a bridge design, which would
shift the pressure outward.

Joseph Bishop and Charles Simonson were called upon to con-
struct it. As two of New York's finest shipbuilders, they had built
dozens of ships for various owners, but even their expertise and
experience were tested by Vanderbilt's ambitious design. Referring to just the plans alone, both men admitted they had never seen
anything like it. Vanderbilt, however, had both a solid reputation
built on several decades in the steamboat industry and the money
to back up his words. Although faced with a daunting task, Bishop
and Simonson were on board 100 percent.

Vanderbilt spared no expense on the inside either, choosing the
finest material and fabrics to complete his floating palace. He
named it *Lexington,* after the start of the Revolutionary War. A
fitting name, given that the boat itself was indeed revolutionary,
especially its steam power source, which as Vanderbilt boasted was
"as perfect an engine as I had ever seen." In April of 1835, Vanderbilt proudly watched the *Lexington* launched to great fanfare
from the East River.

Vanderbilt's builders had faithfully carried out their mission and
created the nation's most opulent passenger ship. The biggest test,
however, would come when the world saw how fast it actually made
it to Rhode Island, a 210-mile voyage that normally took 18 hours
or more. When it finally arrived in Providence, word was sent back.
His exultations that day were warranted: the *Lexington* had made
it in 12 hours! The rival steamboat company could only watch in
astonishment.

The influential business-types quickly countered with plans to
build boats of their own with as much, if not more, firepower
than Vanderbilt's dream machine. Vanderbilt, however, anticipating such a move, had more tricks up his sleeve. His plan was to

Cornelius Vanderbilt. The Library of Congress, part of the Daguerreotype Collection, Mathew B. Brady [1844-1850].

monopolize the market by lowering prices on fares, thereby increasing customers if not revenue. When a new 50-mile railroad line was built between Providence and Stonington, Connecticut, Vanderbilt had even more leverage.

The line began at the far northern end of the Long Island Sound on the Rhode Island border just past Block Island, a small inhabited land mass used by the British during the War of 1812 to dock ships vital to protecting the mouth of the Sound. The newly built Stonington Rail Line, as it came to be called, was a godsend. Not only did it lop off three hours of ocean time from the Sound to Boston, it also offered a far more agreeable commuting experience. Until then, the last part of the journey was around Point Judith and out into an unavoidable, choppy stretch of open water. By the time the boat rocked and rolled its way to the dock in Providence, passengers were green with seasickness. The new railroad line eliminated this by giving riders a choice to exit before Point Judith and take instead a more comfortable trip to Providence in a rail car. One of the first to test the new rail lines, Vanderbilt proclaimed it to be the "fastest route to Boston" and "potentially a key to the entire battle for the Sound," a battle Vanderbilt had seemingly already won.

As was the case with many new rail ventures, the Stonington line was in dire financial straits even before it was built. Millions in stocks and bonds had put it deep in the red, and Vanderbilt knew it would take the startup company years to pay back all the interest. Steamboats were the lifeline for the embattled Stonington, but control over water was just as contentious as on land. The new rail line needed a solid partnership with one of the steamboat lines to ensure a steady flow of fare-paying passengers would be dropped off in Stonington to fill the trains. Vanderbilt had a bargaining chip. If the company did not buy his fastest boat, the *Lexington,* he would keep running it to Providence at a ridiculously low fare of $1, making the complete trip to Boston under $5 per ticket. This was less than Stonington was charging for the privilege of using their rail line alone. It was a shrewd and calculated move by Vanderbilt. The Stonington was too far in debt to stop the line or shut it down. They needed to build capital, not lose it.

Vanderbilt's threat was stifling, and the deal enticing. They needed more than just the one boat, so they balked at first, hoping for a more suitable solution.

As it turned out, the Transportation Company also tried to broker a deal with Stonington. Their tactics, however, were different from Vanderbilt's. They cut off all boats to the Stonington port, hoping to swing the negotiations to their advantage. Their showcase ship, the *J.W. Richmond,* was also earning points for speed. This made for an almost comical rivalry between the *Lexington* and *J.W. Richmond,* which ran schedules to Providence at virtually the same time.

For the Transportation Company, the strike against Stonington proved that time deficiency was costly. Since they weren't offering any cut-rate deals, their customers demanded they return the option of disembarking in Stonington and using the quicker rail line. The Transportation Company was losing the battle. Now they needed the Stonington just as much as Stonington needed the boats. In contrast, Vanderbilt's cheap fare offer was potentially damaging to both companies.

Since it was in everyone's best interest to use the more productive Stonington line, a deal was brokered by the Transportation Company to buy Vanderbilt's *Lexington* for $60,000, with Stonington kicking in another $10,000. It was an outrageous sum for a boat with an original production cost of $75,000 and three years of ocean wear, but they had little choice. In reality, both companies wanted the boat just as much as they wanted Vanderbilt out of the way. They got both–sort of. When the *Lexington* changed hands, the pilot hired to steer her was another Vanderbilt, Jacob or "Jake" as his friends liked to call him, the younger brother of the ship's now former owner.

Even before piloting the *Lexington,* Jacob Vanderbilt was an engaging figure in New York. Together he and his brother owned the *General Jackson,* and Jacob was put in complete charge of the boat's day-to-day operations, like hauling freight and passengers on short jaunts down the Hudson River. Unlike his brother's success, however, the road to his own did not come smoothly. On June

7, 1831, Jacob stood near the bow of the *General Jackson* as the pilot guided the boat to a pier where some 40 passengers were waiting to embark. Jacob was jumping off to load the luggage when he heard a loud boom and was knocked to the ground. The entire engine blew, blasting the boiler from its bolts like a rocket and sending a spray of scalding steam across the pier, killing nine. The bodies of two workers were found sealed to the sunken hull.

Jacob was uninjured, and some might say insensitive, for shortly after the blast he boarded the passing steamboat *Albany* and left. The injured, along with the victims' families, were outraged. They demanded answers. Jacob was forced to write a letter to a New York newspaper, explaining that he fled the scene to seek more help. His half-hearted apology was made even worse when he tried to paint himself a victim too. "I am one-half owner of the *General Jackson*," he wrote, "and by her destruction found myself in one moment stripped of my property and ruined in my prospects." Nothing seemed to quell the anger. *The New York Evening Post* explained that "speed" was a dangerous game in the steamboat industry, even though speed had nothing to do with this particular disaster. The next proclamation was more revealing: "The public mind is painfully aroused to the subject of steamboat explosions."

Jacob would recover from the public scrutiny and work again for his older brother, who would use "Jake's" misfortune on the *General Jackson* to his own clever advantage. Only a week before the blast, Cornelius Vanderbilt had brokered a buyout from his competitors to sell his other boat, *Citizen,* for an inflated price, a move that foreshadowed the sort of deal he would make with the *Lexington* nearly a decade later. The route was hazardous and undesirable, Vanderbilt interjected. So, he sold off his interest and promised not to return. Jacob would be in sole possession of the *General Jackson,* he explained, not him. But now that the *General Jackson* was gone, matters had changed. Realizing too much was at stake, Vanderbilt got back in the game. He used the brokered money to lease another boat, the *Flushing,* to take the *General Jackson's* place. He also built another beauty, the aptly named *Cinderella,* to take over the route permanently. The new owners of the *Citizen* balked, but Vanderbilt chastised them. He made no formal agreement to back off from using other boats as competition. Whether this was merely shrewd gamesmanship on his part or a total lie, there was nothing illegal about what he did. Besides, Vanderbilt argued, he wasn't the only person running steamboats on that line. He was just the one the others were trying to keep away.

2

I saw the upper deck on fire

ᒪᗅ Like his brother Jacob, two years after the *General Jackson* disaster, Cornelius was involved in a bizarre accident of his own, this one on a train rather than a ship. Vanderbilt was traveling by rail between Highstown and Spotswood, New Jersey, when a box containing a wheel bearing blew apart, sending one car on its side, followed by several more. Vanderbilt was badly hurt: he shattered several bones in his leg, cracked a few ribs, and punctured a lung. However, unlike his brother's role in the *General Jackson* explosion, Vanderbilt was only a passenger on the train and bore no responsibility for the outcome. He rarely talked about the wreck until some 40 years later, in 1877, when the incident was brought up again.

Before his death that year at the age of 83, Vanderbilt had sought medicine healers for pain and spiritual mediums for an obsession with contacting the dead. His so-called "skeletons," as the newspapers described them, were exposed in the hearings regarding his will. Vanderbilt had bequeathed $95 million, or nearly all of what he was worth, to his oldest living son, William. Not everyone in the large Vanderbilt family agreed. They held a hearing to determine if Vanderbilt was of sound mind. In question were the injuries suffered in the wreck. Could they have affected his thought process as an older man? In the end, the hearings turned out to be a monumental waste of time. Nothing new was determined about Vanderbilt's sanity other than he became more "irritable" as he got older, something about which his longtime doctor, who was the first to testify, steadfastly agreed.

Conversely, Jacob Vanderbilt had no such fuss when he died in March of 1893. Although he spent years piloting steamboats and managing railroad lines out of Staten Island, he was destined to be just a footnote in the epic life of his famous brother. However, in the context of the *Lexington* story, his presence—or, rather, the lack thereof—plays an intriguing role.

When the *Lexington* pulled out of New York's bay on that fateful night in January, Jacob Vanderbilt was not aboard. Instead, he was at home in bed, sneezing and wheezing with a head cold. Too sick to fulfill his duties, Jacob called on Captain George Child to stand in his stead. So it came to be that Child, a four-year veteran of the Sound who normally served on another company steamer, the *Mohegan,* was in charge of the *Lexington* that night.

Child was different from Jacob, a bit more cautious and a lot less careless. His concern was getting through the dangerous tides of Hell's Gate and the narrows of the East River and out into the often unpredictable waters of the Sound. Once the threat of ice or other hazards had passed, Child could freely attend to captain's business. He greeted each patron with a friendly smile and a tip of the cap and made sure every fare-paying customer, even those who were fearful of steamboats, felt safe.

At 6:00 in the evening, nearly 115 people gathered around the dining tables to raise their glasses and engage in spirited conversation. Among some of the notable passengers on board were a Harvard professor named Dr. Charles Follen, a group of New York bankers, a comedy act from Boston named Eberle and Finn, and several boat captains including Benjamin Foster, who was returning from a three-year sea voyage to India. One man named William Townsend explained he was giving his wife a break by taking their two girls on a trip to Boston himself. Also on board was a family of four: three living, one dead. Alice Winslow, a recent widow, was escorting her husband's dead body back to Boston, so she could bury him in the family plot. Her husband's father and brother accompanied her on the trip. Another woman, Mary Russell, had just been married the day before and was traveling to Boston to deliver the news of her recent matrimony to her parents.

Captain Child likely told them all how the danger of ice had passed and the serene waters that lay ahead posed no concern. All was well. The trip was progressing smoothly and the ship was gloriously accommodating, with its warm boilers creating a cozy environment inside while the frigid bite of winter raged just beyond the portholes.

January 13, 1834, 7:30 P.M.

Outside on the deck, first a spark, then flames, quickly ignited the tightly wound cotton bales. The *Lexington* was soon consumed by fire and smoke. Idle curiosity swiftly gave way to sheer panic. Passengers had no choice but to face the excruciating fate of being burnt alive or jumping into the freezing waters. Few knew how to swim, but even for those who did, there was next to no chance of survival. The faint light of the visible shoreline two miles away was too far to make before succumbing to the cold. This did not prevent land dwellers on the Connecticut side from attempting an impromptu rescue. Fishermen launched their boats in a desperate attempt to save those struggling in the water. Fearing the worst, they soon found ice packs blocking the inlets as the winds and shifting tide kept sending the burning *Lexington* back to the center of the Sound.

The captain of the docked steamer *Merchant,* Oliver Meeker, could see the orange glow in the distance. He also gave it a go, but found the water too shallow due to the falling tide. All anyone could do from the shore was watch in horror as the flames flickered out and the screams faded. When dawn finally arrived, Captain Meeker lightened the load on the *Merchant* and with the incoming tide was able to slip off the sandy shoreline and lumber through the ice and debris. No one had expected to find any survivors, but soon several bales of cotton were spotted bobbing in the water. Miraculously on top were figures, feebly managing to wave handkerchiefs that they had used to keep their hands warm through the night. They were picked up, one to a bale, but only three in all. They were all boatmen: two crewmembers of the ill-fated ship and another captain, named Chester Hillard, who had been traveling back home after being at sea for months.

Stephen Manchester, the pilot of the ship, was one of the three rescued. His story was similar to the other survivors. Once he realized there was no choice but to jump, he landed first on a "stage or raft"–likely just a floating board–and managed to stay mostly dry. From there he hopped on a floating bale. Another man managed to mount the bale too, but he had been in the icy water first. His clothes were soaked and the chill eventually sucked the life out of him. Manchester said he watched the man die and drift off.

Manchester, now alone, had nearly succumbed to frostbite by the time the *Merchant* picked him up. Soon he had a story to tell. The stacked cotton bales close to the smoke stacks caught fire, he described. He watched it all unfold from the pilothouse: "I saw the upper deck on fire, all around the smoke pipe and blazing up two or three feet perhaps, above the promenade deck. The flame seemed to be a thin sheet, and apparently, just commenced. I again went into the wheel house, caught hold of the wheel, hove it hard a port, and steered the boat head to land." Manchester tried to turn the boat but found the wheel didn't respond. Several men tried to help. They gripped and pulled down on the wheel, but it spun wildly out of their hands. The fire had cut the steering rope just below the pilothouse.

In the engine room, the crew was forced to evacuate before they could shut down the boilers. The *Lexington* was ablaze, but still moving along at a brisk pace. When the lifeboats hit the water, the force of the waves created by the speeding ship crushed them against the hull. Without boats to save them, passengers chose to take their chances in the water rather than stay on the burning ship. Either way, they were doomed. Once their clothes became saturated, it was only a matter of time before the chilling sea water would suffocate them. Only a small number of cotton bales and a smattering of floating debris offered some hope. Another crewmember, a fireman named Charles Smith, was rescued after lying lengthwise on a paddlewheel plank like a surfboard.

The final survivor, second mate David Crowley, was only 20 years

"Capt. Manchester and McKenna on the bale of cotton." From *Steamboat disasters and railroad accidents in the United States* by S.A. Howland [1846].

old. Like some of the others, he had first found a plank and then later commandeered a drifting bale. He burrowed a hole in the center of the bale and climbed in, stuffing his clothes with the extra cotton for warmth. When the bale drifted close enough to the ice packs, he crawled across the slippery surface until he reached the shore. In the distance he could make out the faint light of a home. A man named Mathias Hutchinson found Crowley at his doorstep, shivering and looking like a corpse. He sat him by the warm fire until he revived enough to talk. When Crowley told his harrowing story, Hutchinson related to him that if his timeline was correct, he had been on his makeshift raft for nearly 48 hours. He was also 50 miles from where the *Lexington* went down. He had little hope for any survivors. In fact, he fearfully speculated that he might be the only one. In all, an estimated 140 people on board the stricken ship lost their lives that night.

When the news of the *Lexington* finally reached New York City, grieving families demanded answers and immediately an inquiry took place. Blame was thrown at the owners for running a dangerous ship and the dockworkers for grossly miscalculating the combustibility of the tightly packed cotton bales. The crew in general, and especially Captain Child, were all posthumously cited for dereliction of duty, though the three surviving members, including Captain Manchester, were eventually exonerated.

But placing blame on the crew wasn't the public's only concern. On board the *Lexington* was nearly $70,000 in coins and bank notes. Most of the paper notes were likely destroyed, but the silver coins were a different matter. It depended how quickly they made it into the water. While this wasn't the concern of the grieving families, the bank managers whose money was aboard the ship—now either burned, missing, or sitting at the bottom of the Sound—had questions for one man: William Harnden.

William Frederick Harnden was born in 1812 in Reading, Massachusetts. His father was a house painter, and had young William not been so slight in stature, he might have picked up on the trade, too. Instead, Harnden went to work for the railroad. He spent years as a train conductor and ticket agent, watching passengers drop off packages for transfer and assuming someone else would be responsible enough to get them there. Whether they actually did or not, however, was never guaranteed. This was not a contentious issue for less expensive items like candy or clothing, but the safe arrival of more valuables keepsakes, such as jewelry and watches, was more significant. This usually meant the owners of the pieces would travel with their valuables themselves to ensure their safe arrival.

Harnden could see the potential of a package delivery service. He immediately sent letters promoting his idea to steamer companies on the Sound and train lines running between Providence and Boston. He also met with a railroad man named Mr. Moore, a conductor on the Boston and Worchester railroad. Harnden asked if he would like to be a partner in the business. Moore refused at first and instead sought to seek the express business on his own. Moore's first inquiry at the office of the Superintendent of the Boston to Providence line turned out to be the most damaging: Harnden had gotten there first. The partnership deal was off.

With a railroad line contract secured, Harnden offered customers a different approach to express service. Now passengers could leave their packages with him, and he would see to it that their valuables made the journey, safe and secure. From drop-off to delivery, the goods would be protected, Harnden ensured. But the everyday paying passenger was just one potential customer and Harnden's expectation for his business was limitless. So when Harnden went to New York City to shore up a customer base, he met with bankers and investors and pitched his idea. Essentially, he told them, he was going to Providence and Boston by steamer and rail and they could pay him to guard their important letters, contracts, coins, or greenbacks during transit. In addition, he would pick up the goods and deliver them too. Soon, bank executives were clamoring for Harnden's service and in February of 1838, the Harnden Express opened an office on Wall Street. The *Boston Transcript* was high on praise. "It affords us much pleasure to recommend the express to the notice of our readers," they reported. "[The Express] is highly convenient for those who wish to send small packages from one city to the other."

But with money came great risk. On that cold Monday evening in January, aboard the doomed *Lexington,* Harnden had been entrusted with $20,000 on behalf of Franklin Havin, President of the Merchants Bank. The money was put in an iron box, or portable safe. Some of the currency was in coin, perhaps as much as $12,000 worth of silver pieces. Harnden had personally supervised the packing and sent his best messenger, his younger brother Adolphus, to make sure of its safekeeping.

The news was bad on all fronts. Not only had there been a significant loss of life on the *Lexington,* but most of the passengers' belongings were assumed missing or destroyed as well. Harnden's protected safe, however, was another matter. If it had gone down with the ship, many speculated, perhaps it may yet be recovered and the silver coins saved. The salvage operation, though, was for the recovery of bodies first. The search for the safe would come second, if at all.

After two days, numerous sections of the wreckage were found but only seven bodies were recovered or washed up on shore. Attempts to raise the ship eight months later were only mildly successful. "The wreck of this ill-fated vessel has been raised to the surface," reported the *Long Islander,* a weekly newspaper in Huntington, New York. But the ship's burnt-out shell wasn't above the water for long. "One of the chains broke and the *Lexington* went down again, this time back to its final resting place, 130 feet below, and this time for good."

Apparently, Harnden's protected loot went with it.

3

Sorry, no silver

 Raising shipwrecks was not an easy task. Even today, remnants of ships which suffered a similar fate as the *Lexington* still sit in their watery graves. Dozens, if not hundreds, lie untouched. Divers may discover them by accident, but that's rare. Only expensive and extensive expeditions undertaken at sites where the wreck's cargo may still be salvable are even mildly successful. These modern-day ship hunters have the stories, locations, and equipment to search for the lost treasure, though in most cases little of value is found. Generally, sunken ships were just left entombed on the bottom to become part of the underwater landscape. Since raising them was time-consuming and costly, it was simply not worth the effort. Later, in the advent of more sophisticated diving equipment such as the diving bell, recovering precious cargo like rum, coins, or ammunition became more plausible, even expected. However, before this breakthrough technology, only what rose to the surface willingly—including victims' remains—were salvageable. Yet, when something valuable or indispensable was on board, efforts were made to recover the loss, regardless of the cost.

In 1782, a large warship HMS *Royal George* was set to sail for Gibraltar when it took on water, tipped over, and quickly sank near the island city of Portsmouth, England, in a strait known as Spithead. More than 800 crewmembers and their families—who ironically were on board, saying goodbye to their loved ones—perished in the accident. King George III immediately ordered the *Royal George* be brought back up. The ship's 100 heavy iron cannons and guns were too important to leave resting for eternity in the harbor.

Usually such an order, even a royal one, was pointless. The ship would be buried in too deep of water to even consider recovering, but in the case of the *Royal George*, circumstances were different. The ship was in the channel and still near the shore when it fell over. Thus, it was just barely submerged. When the *Royal George* hit bottom, the top of the mast was only slightly below the surface. The King demanded his cannons back. *But how?* No one had ever attempted such an undertaking. The King offered a handsome monetary reward to anyone who could devise a system to bring the ship and its cargo back to the surface.

According to a report, 117 proposals were received and among these a local ship broker named William Tracey was chosen. His plan involved using cables, cradles, and several smaller ships to secure the wreck, then waiting for a low tide to pull the slack, and see the tide rise again. "Either the two top ships would sink," Tracey surmised, "or the wreck would lift." A trial run was promising, but when all the lines were secured, weather foiled each attempt. Heavy gale winds kept pushing the top boats and snapping the cables. Eventually, the British Navy lost patience. "No further assistance can be given to you," they responded when Tracey asked for more funds. Even the enticing offer to recover some of the ship's store of rum for payment was rescinded. Tracey, who had spent a good portion of his own money hoping to cash in, pleaded for a chance to keep trying. Eventually he gave up asking, absorbed his personal loses, and quit.

The *Royal George* was never raised.

No such efforts were made with the *Lexington*, however. The ship's burnt-out shell sat buried and undisturbed in the middle of the Long Island Sound until April 1983, when a salvage crew searched the area where it went down. They found the wreck site and remains of the ship. "The length of the burned and broken hull, the great paddlewheels, the walking beams of the engines are more imagined than seen," wrote Clive Cussler in his book *The Sea Hunters: True Adventures with Famous Shipwrecks.* "The dismal green, murky waters allow only a few closeup glimpses of how the ship must have once appeared. You feel as if you're groping through a haunted house at night, glimpsing ghosts from the corner of the eye."

The *Lexington* was found in three broken sections. A few artifacts like loose bolts and charred wood were discovered, but nothing of importance or value. "Sorry, no silver," Cussler writes. As it turned out, divers in the 18th century had better luck. "Recovered from her was a lump of silver, melded coins, weighing about thirty pounds and estimated to be worth $800," the papers reported. This was only a fraction of the total coin value on board, but at least Harnden could say his messenger carried out his duty that day.

Since Adolphus Harnden wasn't around to tell his side of the story, one of the survivors, Captain Manchester, spoke for him. When asked in an inquiry, Manchester claimed Adolphus was one of the last men to leave the ship. This would seem to confirm the messenger stayed with the loot, protecting it until he had no other choice than to jump.

In his book written in 1858 about the history of express companies, T.J. Stimson spins a tale of Harnden's bravery on board the *Lexington* that night: "Express managers have, in numerous instances of disasters by sea and land distinguished themselves by their presence of mind and intrepidity in seeking to save or serve those in distress around them," Stimson writes. "In Harnden's case any attempt to rescue his fellow passengers would be futile. His only card was for the safety of the very heavy amount of treasure in his charge." The next passage describing Harnden's actions is complete hearsay, taken presumably only from Manchester's testimony: "He [Harnden] took his iron safe, containing about $40,000 from the crate before the [life] boats were swamped in hopes of getting them into one of them, after they had done their office in conveying passengers and others ashore. Finding it was too heavy for that, he may have opened and taken it out for their better conveyance." Since the life boats were irrelevant in the wreck, the account is frivolous at best. Furthermore, since no firsthand accounts existed of Harnden's actions that night, Stimson's story makes for good theater only. "That he behaved with courage and fortitude, we have no reason to doubt," Stimson finishes with a flourish.

Stimson's praise of the Harnden Express Company, however, was more justifiable. The day after the *Lexington* disaster, another steamer, the *Providence,* set sail for Connecticut on the same route. Due to severe ice, it would be the last boat to cross the dangerous waters for several weeks, but it was significant in another regard. On board the *Providence* was a man named E.J. Stone, a messenger for Harnden's express service. Stone, who "seems to have stood ready," was Adolphus's replacement. Without missing a beat, William Harnden was back protecting more valuables and currency aboard the steamers. Stimson explains Harnden's resolve this way: "Put a wall of fire between New York and Boston, and he would have tunneled the solid earth, but he would have got his express through."

Harnden's persistence in the face of adversity paid off. In 1846, just six years after the *Lexington* disaster and only a year after his sudden death from consumption at the age of 33, the "father of the express business" was lauded for his short but celebrated accomplishments. "[Harnden's] success was far beyond his expectations; and before he died, he had succeeded in establishing branches of his establishment in London, Liverpool, Paris, Havre, and many other places of magnitude in Great Britain and on the continent," wrote London's *True Sun.*

4
Bring back
materials

 In New York City, not far from Harnden's messenger service office on the eight-block-long stretch of road named after a
defensive 12-foot barrier built in 1652 by Dutch settlers to keep the
English and anyone else who might do them harm from entering
an area near the colony's harbor, a young lithographer had set up
a business in a distinctive address even to this day: 1 Wall Street.

His name was Nathaniel Currier.

Many great ideas and discoveries were influenced by the failures
and missteps of those who came before them. Nathaniel Currier
was no exception. His name would become synonymous with a
product as popular as any for its time. His personal story, however,
is not as well-known. It begins with another catastrophe, another
destructive fire. On the evening of December 16, 1835, a watchman
named William Hayes was patrolling the financial district close to
Currier's Wall Street office when he smelled smoke. A large ware-
house had caught fire at the corner of Exchange and Pearl Streets.
Nearby, several commercial businesses were threatened.

The winter's night was particularly raw, and gusty winds blew
through the city streets. Hydrants froze. Attempts were made to
break holes in the frozen East River to extract water, but that
took precious time. Merchant owners who feared the worst ran to
their businesses and tried to salvage goods by tossing them into

the streets. Looting soon followed. Encountering little resistance and fueled by the high winds, the fire kept spreading. Spectators watched in disbelief as some of the city's largest and most important financial institutions, including the three-storied Merchant Exchange on the south side of Wall Street, went up in flames. Most of the major newspaper offices in town also succumbed to the massive blaze.

Charles King, editor of the *New York American,* arrived to find workers trying to move equipment out, but once the fire reached the building, it was gone in 15 minutes. King rushed to find the mayor. He had an idea: if they purposely blew up several buildings before the fire arrived, the burnt piles might suppress the fire's movement. In addition, the implosions would help eliminate walls and rooftops where flying embers easily attached. One by one, they set powder kegs in the cellars of buildings along the fire's path, and one by one the buildings were blown to the ground. Others fell simply from the shockwaves of another crashing down.

King's plan worked, but the damage was extensive. "We write with the evidences of calamity around us so extensive that history hardly furnishes a parallel to it," the *Evening Post* reported the next morning. The building which housed the *Post* was saved, but the *"Daily, Gazette* and *American* are all burned down and will not appear today." The loss of property–and perhaps lives, the paper noted–would be unfathomable: "Hence it is our account, thus imperfect to estimate the amount of property lost is impractical, but it must be millions upon millions." In the end, though the tally was large, the death toll was not. The fire covered nearly 17 city blocks, destroying 700 buildings–nearly all businesses–but killing only two. While lives were mostly spared, livelihoods were not. Many residents who had businesses or housed expensive items along the devastated route were left with nothing to show for it, no insurance, and no goods to resell. "Many of our fellow citizens, who retired to their pillows in affluence, were bankrupt on awaking," the papers reported the next day.

But not Nathaniel Currier. The little printing shop at 1 Wall Street and the two small presses inside remained untouched. In fact, the devastating fire turned out to be an unsuspecting boon

for Currier and his lithograph business. Four days after the blaze
and while the impact of the devastation was still sinking in, Currier had a print to sell.

Currier had set a dramatic scene on stone, then paper. It showed
the front of the exchange building still intact while the rest was in
ruins. Several firemen are standing beside it, one holding a hose
that sags in his arms, perhaps symbolizing that the building is lost
or representing that he is waiting for precious water to arrive. Fire
and smoke continue to billow in the background. The sketch is
attributed to J.H. Bufford, a friend of Currier, who moved to New
York and together with Currier published mostly music and man-
ual prints at the time; that is, until the fire came along. The print,
titled "Ruins of the Merchant Exchange N.Y. After the Destructive Conflagration of Dec 16 & 17, 1835," sold well and Currier's
business took off.

Then in May of that same year, word arrived in New York City of
another disaster, this time in New Orleans. "The Planter's Hotel
Fell to the Earth," the story read. "There were 50 persons in the
building at the time. About 40 miraculously escaped with their
lives, many of whom received not the slightest of injury. The remainder was buried in the ruins." This was no fire, but instead a
colossal collapse caused by ongoing repairs to the lower level of
the three-story structure. The *Evening Post* speculated that much
of the support had been "incautiously cut away." The distinctive
cracks of wood heard before the building crumbled to the ground
sounded like a small cannon to one observer. "There was a sound
like an earthquake as the mass fell," the papers noted. Once again,
Currier set a Bufford drawing to paper, this time showing a wide
shot of the hotel building in ruins while a large crowd gathers in
the street like a festival. "Ruins of the Planters Hotel in New Orleans" proved to be another good seller.

As it turned out, the scenes depicting the devastating New York
fire and the hotel disaster in New Orleans were just a precursor to
what was to follow for the young printer on Wall Street. Another
disaster would soon befall the city, and because of it, Currier, the
brand, would become nationally famous.

"Ruins of the Merchant's Exchange New York". The Library of Congress, published by Nathaniel Currier [1835].

Currier did not invent this new medium called lithography, nor was he the first to capitalize on it. A Bavarian named Alois Senefelder is credited with introducing the printing process to the French in 1816. Senefelder's idea was simple, yet ingenious. First, using a thin layer of sand and rock, a stone surface is ground over until it is velvety smooth. Next, a fine instrument composed of wax or something equally water-resistant is used to create a design on the face of the stone. After the design or lettering is made, the stone is given a bath of gum. The parts covered by wax pencil stick out in low relief. The stone is now put in a roller and lithographic ink is applied, which, according to one source, then consisted of "beef suet, goose grease, white wax, castile soap, gum mastic, shellac, and gas black." As the roller passes over the plate, the greasy ink picks up the wax impression and repels the wet stone. Paper is then applied to the inked plate and prints are made.

In 1819, a portrait painter named Bass Otis is credited with making the first lithographic print in America. A woodland scene consisting of "a single house upon the bank of a river" appeared in *The Analectic Magazine* in July of that year. Not much credit is given to Otis for its invention. The magazine article only explains that Otis had the stone imported from Munich and presented it to the American Philosophical Society. Nevertheless, he is heralded for pioneering a new process. "In this number we present to our readers a specimen of *American Lithography,*" the article read. That, however, was it for Otis' lithography career: only one other lithographic print is credited to him in 1820.

Inspired either by Otis' work in the article or the prints that were being produced overseas, other craftsmen picked up the slack. Among them were the brothers John and William Pendleton, who opened the first lithography studio in Boston and gained public acceptance for their work. The Pendletons are credited with expanding the printing business in the U.S., but as so often happens, the brothers have another man to thank for their interest in lithography.

In 1786, Charles Willson Peale ran a successful museum in Philadelphia. One of the first of its kind, the natural history museum housed specimens, mostly stuffed or dried animals. These included more than 1,000 birds, 4,000 insects, 200 snakes, and one Angora cat, described as "badly preserved."

Eventually, showman P.T. Barnum bought out the museum after Charles retired and left the day-to-day operations to his six sons. Charles was also a notable portrait artist and named one of his boys Rembrandt after the famous 17th-century Dutch painter. Although Charles taught all his sons how to paint, the aptly named Rembrandt showed the most promise. By the age of 13, he had made a self-portrait which was not only strikingly accomplished for a teenager, but also highly unusual. Rembrandt had painted himself looking much older and perhaps more handsome too, with curls described as of that of a "Renaissance angel." Later, Rembrandt would show his first work to students as a teaching tool, explaining "this is how you can go from bad to better."

In July of 1787, Charles introduced Rembrandt, now 17, to General George Washington. The association between the elder Peale and the general is not fully known. Perhaps Washington was an admirer of Peale's newly opened history museum. Regardless, the general wanted his portrait painted and Charles was an artist. So Charles painted Washington as Rembrandt watched. Then, in 1795, the 25-year-old Rembrandt was summoned to the nation's capital—this time, alone.

Washington, now serving his sixth of an eventual eight years as the country's first president, must have remembered the earlier sitting. He invited Rembrandt to paint his likeness just as Charles had done nearly a decade before. As he did with his own self-portrait, Rembrandt made Washington look slightly older than his 63 years. Washington liked it and the portrait of the president sitting in a black overcoat with a thin-lipped expression and rosy cheeks was well-received in art circles. Rembrandt, however, was not satisfied. He felt he had done a disservice to the nation by not painting Washington in a more patriotic and appealing light. So in 1832, 33 years after Washington's death, he painted the president again, this time in full military uniform and with a more youthful and heroic stare. Rembrandt also had the new likeness copied, now possible because of lithography.

Rembrandt Peale. The Library of Congress, F. De B. (Frederick De Bourg)
Richards, photographer [1855-1860].

In 1814, Rembrandt, like his father before him, opened a museum in Baltimore. Instead of stuffed birds, however, Peale displayed only art. Here William and John Pendleton reenter the story. The Pendleton brothers, who worked as "men-of-all-work" at Charles' Philadelphia museum, did the same for Rembrandt as well. It is said they helped Rembrandt install gaslights at the new museum. This must have fueled their interest in experimental lithography. Rembrandt was already familiar with the early stages of the process, having traveled to Europe in 1802 to study with another artist, Benjamin West, who had lithographs of some of his own work done.

There are more questions than answers as to why the Pendletons ended up in Boston and opened the first lithography shop in the U.S. John was reportedly in England while William was just getting established in the port city when he received or bought lithograph stones from an overseas merchant who didn't know what to do with them. William wrote to his brother. "Bring back materials," he urged. John did even better. He brought back a printer, a man named Dubois, who is credited with being the first pressman in the U.S. "He [Dubois] has studied in the best printing-houses Paris houses, and has commenced his practice here, well furnished with knowledge and materials to pursue it to advantage," raved the *United States Literary Gazette*. "We hope his skill and enterprise will meet with the encouragement for which they so eminently deserve." Some suggest William himself wrote the complimentary article to shamelessly promote their own self-interest. Regardless, the Pendletons' shop not only became a successful printing business, but also a training ground for a number of potential artists and printmakers eager to learn the trade.

One young apprentice was Nathaniel Currier, a 15-year-old who expressed a great interest in lithography as a career. With a wealth of knowledge he accrued from the brothers' instruction, the young protégé would branch out on his own, first opening a small shop in Philadelphia, then moving on to New York City to set up another lithograph business before the Pendletons could. At first, Currier worked with several partners, printing transcribed manuscripts and music pieces. This garnered a steady income for Currier, who was looking for more challenges—and more business. In 1835, when the great New York fire broke out, that all changed. Currier had found a profitable niche and willing customer base in the disaster prints. Moreover, the speed by which Currier and his artist could produce such a print proved even more crucial. Now readers' imaginations could soar with a vivid rendition of a horrific scene within days, not months.

5

A genius
and an ass

C→ The *New York Sun* was the first newspaper to recognize
the power of juxtaposing words and images when telling a devastating tale such as the *Lexington* disaster. Shortly after the smoke
cleared and the news of the terrible calamity had reached the city,
an extra edition of the paper appeared: a standalone sheet, which
included a Nathaniel Currier print and seven columns of letter-
press describing the accident. The image took up nearly half of the
page and was just as realistic as the stories that preceded it. In the
background, the doomed vessel is seen afloat. A large ball of fire
occupies its middle, burning in a fury of flames that seem to shoot
beyond the top of the picture. Frantic figures line the rails, destined soon either to jump or be pushed into the icy waters. In the
foreground, passengers cling to bales of cotton dotting the choppy
waters in front of the ship. The only lifeboat to be seen hangs pre-
cariously near the stern; its bow is dipped, touching the water. Passengers in the lifeboat hold up their arms in despair. In the water,
one man perched on a bale reaches out to another person, presumably a woman, in a desperate attempt to save her life.

The rendition was a glorious, realistic, and violent snapshot of
an actual event, made all the more powerful given that readers
knew the awful fate awaiting each and every person dramatized in
the drawing. The *Extra Sun,* as the single sheet was called, was a

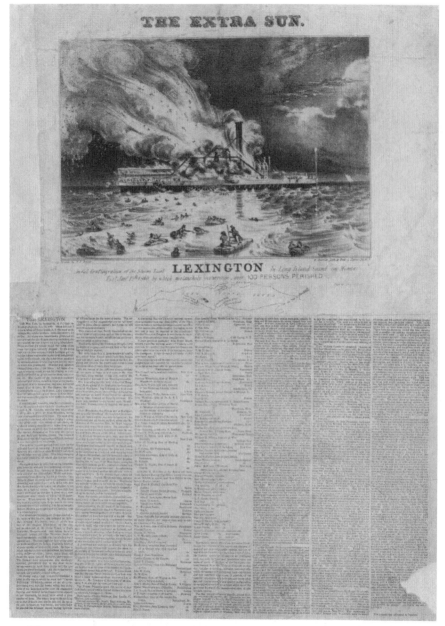

"Lexington Disaster", *The Extra Sun*. Public Domain.

big sensation. Street newsboys couldn't keep them in their hands, despite the lithograph's convoluted title: "The Awful Conflagration of the Steam Boat Lexington in Long Sound on Monday Eveg. Jany. 13th 1840, by which melancholy occurrence over 100 persons perished." The artist's name was William Keesey Hewitt, a portraitist from Philadelphia, whose relative James L. Hewitt was a music publisher who worked closely with Currier. Not much else is known about Hewitt, other than his work which includes another Currier print of George Washington crossing the Delaware—not the more famous one of Washington standing in a ship, flanked by American flags, by Emanuel Gottlieb Leutze in 1852—but one instead of the general on horseback cantering through the shallow water. The *Lexington* drawing was by far Hewitt's most popular piece. It sold well, not just in New York, but in other cities as well. Currier, however, would get most of the credit. Fine works of art were being produced and hung in museums for a select few to enjoy, but the process of lithography was accessible to thousands.

Currier had become a household name.

Currier, however, had another person to thank for his success: Moses Beach, the editor of the *Sun*. Beach approached Currier with the novel idea of putting a lithograph print in his paper, but Currier had to be quick. News had already trickled into the city by Wednesday, two days after the disaster, and Beach wanted the extra edition out by the weekend.

Born into a modest farm family in Connecticut, Moses Yale Beach was a tinkerer and inventor who created such industrial machines as a gunpowder engine to launch balloons and a rag-cutting machine for paper mills. For reasons unknown, the balloon launcher failed to catch on, but the rag-picker was widely used. Unfortunately for Beach, he never patented the idea and therefore procured no financial rewards for its success. Undeterred, he moved on and bought a paper mill and eventually became a rich man, though bad investments in the coming years would diminish his wealth considerably and force him to abandon the businesses. Despite this, he still found someone to love him.

Nancy Day turned out to be the sister of Benjamin Day, the editor of the *New York Sun*. Beach, by marriage, was now in the newspaper business. He bought a small stake in the fledging paper in 1835 and eventually bought the business outright three years later for $40,000. It was a failing enterprise at first and Beach hoped to sell, but he stuck with it. Perhaps seeing the future in newspaper reporting, he began to emphasize speed rather than accuracy. He expanded the four-page paper from three columns per page to eight and built a large pigeon house on top the paper's offices at Nassau and Fulton Streets. The carrying birds would receive and return dispatches from ships outside the harbors. As far as Beach was concerned, the sooner news got to the sanctum of the newsroom, the better. It was this kind of thinking that drew him to propose his revolutionary idea to a young lithographer. There was a disaster in town and curious imaginations abounded.

Even after the paper edition ran out, the *Lexington* print remained so popular that Currier ran his presses day and night to keep up with demand. Currier soon earned a national reputation and a slew of new clients. Like Beach, Currier possessed a keen sense of the sensationalism the public wanted—almost tabloid-like stories, accompanied by strikingly graphic images. "Yellow journalism," or sensationalist reporting, was just beginning to explode on the scene and Beach, his predecessor Day, and another newspaper editor, James Gordon Bennett of the *New York Herald,* were at the forefront.

Bennett was especially brash, once boldly comparing his newspaper to nothing less than the Creator himself. "A newspaper can send more souls to heaven, and save more from Hell, than all the churches and chapels in New York," he said, adding, "besides making money at the same time."

Bennett wasn't interested in just telling the stories of grisly murders, suicides, and unfortunate accidents; he was interested in solving them, too. This would seem to point him on the path to journalistic immortality. However, as macabre and manipulative as his work was, Bennett would later be upstaged by a man who arguably made the editorial bias of the press indispensable: William Randolph Hearst. All that would come much later. In fact, by the time Hearst came into the world in April of 1863, Bennett was already

78 and had only nine more years to live. By then he had earned a reputation, as one historian put it, as both a "genius and an ass." So while the Hearst name may have made more history books, Bennett, the forerunner of sensationalist reporting, has the distinction of being called the "Father of Yellow Journalism."

Born in Scotland, Bennett immigrated to the United States in 1819 at the age of 24, ostensibly to see the birthplace of his hero, Benjamin Franklin. The true reason, however, likely had more to do with his overbearing family who tried to push Bennett into the priesthood, something he was adamantly against. He responded by sailing across the Atlantic, never to return.

Bennett spent most of his first decade in America as a freelance writer, eventually landing a job at the *New York Enquirer* in 1827. He made a name and reputation for himself by skewing government "bigotry" and poking fun at everyday social pretentions. Blunt and biting, Bennett didn't care who he offended. In one dispatch, he ridiculed the looks of an unsuspecting—and mercifully nameless—woman whose only crime was simply waiting at a corner long enough for Bennett to take a closer look. "The caputography of her head," he wrote, "would puzzle a corps of engineers." Bennett quickly realized his cutthroat and take-no-prisoners style was wearing thin at the *Enquirer*. With about every other newspaper editor in town despising him, he set off on his own. With an initial grubstaking budget of $500, he found a discreet basement office on Wall Street and began the *New York Herald,* another "one cent" newspaper or "Penny Press." Immediately, Bennett was up to his old tricks, trying to solve crimes before the authorities did. The more scandalous the story, Bennett soon found out, the better it sold. One story, thanks to its infamous connection to writer Edgar Allan Poe, particularly stands out.

Not far from Currier's printing office at the corner of Wall Street and Broadway was a popular cigar shop run by a man named John Anderson. Curious men would frequent Anderson's Tobacco Emporium every day not because Anderson had the best cigars, but because a pretty counter attendant named Mary Rogers worked inside. Bennett's *Herald* made Rogers an instant celebrity by picking up on her demurring sentiments and exploiting them.

Mary's effect was intoxicating, the paper reported, because she was such an innocent flower. "She moved amid the bland perfume," a poem published in the *Herald* read, "her eyes had starlight's azure gloom."

The unmarried 18-year-old Mary, a New York transplant from Connecticut, may have enjoyed the attention, but her instant stardom was also a curse. On October 6, 1838, Mary went missing. Phoebe, her mother, claimed she found a suicide note from her daughter where they both lived, in a boardinghouse on Nassau Street. This time, Bennett and the *Herald* weren't alone; just about every major publication in the city covered the mysterious disappearance of the popular "cigar girl."

As it turned out, Mary was fine. She returned home safely and reports claimed she may have only visited a friend in Brooklyn for the day, possibly only for a few hours. The suicide note was never explained. While the story had a happy ending, the resolution wasn't satisfying enough for inquisitive journalists. Was it a hoax? Had the cigar shop owner John Anderson put Mary up to the stunt for publicity? Was it a pushy suitor who prompted the "cigar girl" to suddenly vanish, then reappear again?

Very little about Mary's brief disappearance was answered. Mary resumed her work at the cigar shop as if nothing had happened. Three years later, she would be back in the news again, this time with a shockingly bizarre twist.

While Currier's *Lexington* print was not the first drawing to appear in a major city publication, it was both the most elaborate and largest print ever to be published on a front page. Until then, newspapers like Beach's *Sun* and Bennett's *Herald* ran crudely drawn depictions of the stories gracing its pages. The *Lexington* cover, however, did not appear in a daily, so the process could take more time. Thus, it wasn't the drawing itself, per se, but the speed by which Currier produced it and Beach published that made it groundbreaking. Beach would get the credit, but it didn't change the game. Until more advanced printing machines and the advent of photography came along a decade later, simple drawings or wood engravings continued to be used sparingly on the pages of

James Gordon Bennett. The Library of Congress, part of the Daguerreotype Collection, Mathew B. Brady [1851-1852].

the Penny Press newspapers. But as the crafty Bennett proved with his coverage in the *Herald,* he didn't have to show a drawing of a story to exploit it. Now, with the latest news about the infamous cigar girl, Bennett would reveal just how influential and deceptive a newspaper could be.

Mary Rogers wasn't just missing…

She was dead.

6

I have a proposition to make

⌒⌒⌒ Elysian Fields was a popular park off the Hudson River with tree-lined pathways and a natural spring known as Sybil's Cave, whose waters, the locals claimed, had "healthful, restorative properties." On August 3, 1841, a strange object was spotted floating there, about 200 to 300 yards from the shore. It wasn't until a rowboat was dispatched that the shocking discovery was revealed. This was no ordinary object: the dress, bonnet on the head, and "light gloves" on the hands confirmed that this was the body of a young woman.

A reporter for Bennett's *Herald* just happened to be nearby when the corpse was brought to shore. "Her forehead and face appeared to have been battered and butchered to a mummy," he wrote. More passersby arrived, including two men who stopped to help. "My God," one man proclaimed after ripping the sleeve of the dead woman's dress and gently caressing her arm, "this is Mary Rogers!" The two men explained they once resided at the boardinghouse Mary and her mother still called home.

Bennett wasted no time in making the coverage his own. He immediately rebuked the competency of the authorities to solve the case and without justification started naming names—suspects he alone felt may have been responsible for the poor woman's death.

One of the names mentioned was Mary's fiancé, Daniel Payne. Other papers like the *Sun, Times,* and *Evening Star* also pointed the finger at Payne, telling an unsubstantiated story of unrequited love, followed by jealous rage. Had Payne seen Mary with another man? The papers ratcheted up the speculation by observing Payne's only alibi for Mary's disappearance was that he had taken a three-hour nap.

A despondent Payne professed innocence but fueled even more speculation when, in October of 1842, he was found lifeless on a park bench near Sybil's Cave, the same spot Mary's body was brought to shore. He was suspected of consuming a bottle of poison after going on a two-day drunken binge. His apparent suicide, however, did not close the case. Payne was no longer a suspect. Earlier, he had been questioned by authorities and vindicated of any wrongdoing in Mary's death, so only the papers kept his involvement alive. Why he killed himself was anyone's guess, but he was most certainly dead.

So Bennett turned his attention to the notorious New York City gangs instead. Perhaps they were involved, he theorized, a plausible yet far-reaching assessment. Bennett, however, had other targets, including the judge assigned to the case, the Honorable Gilbert Merritt, and the New York City police department, whose alleged incompetency served a frequent target for Bennett's paper. In the end, while it made for a sordid tale, Bennett could not break the case and the Mary Rogers murder remained unsolved.

Enter Edgar Allan Poe.

The young poet had just finished a short story "The Murders in the Rue Morgue" in 1841, the year of Mary Rogers' death. Considered to be the "first modern detective story," Poe introduced the French detective C. Auguste Dupin to solve the case of two missing girls, both of whom turned up beaten to death near their home on Rue Morgue, a fictional Parisian street. "To this horrible mystery," Poe wrote in the story, quoting the Paris newspaper *Gazette des Tribunaux,* "there is not as yet, we believe, the slightest clew." Dupin, the first in a line of more famous literary detectives to come, cleverly solved the case. Readers loved it, yet critics were indifferent, though they praised its ingenuity if nothing else.

A year after his story was published, Poe was searching for another case for his fictional detective to tackle.

He chose Mary Rogers.

Why Poe decided to write a second Dupin detective story based on the case of Mary Rogers is left to conjecture. Poe had spent a short time in New York before moving his family to Philadelphia, where Bennett's coverage of the Mary Rogers murder in the *Herald* was reprinted in the *Saturday Evening Post*. In the paper, Bennett had presented the murder of the cigar girl as a "puzzle" for readers to unravel. This may well have intrigued Poe, who had received some criticism for "Rue Morgue" being clever, but contrived. Since Poe had invented the story, readers were only absorbing his thoughts, his clues, and finally his solution. The tale and conclusion, therefore, were already a preordained notion. Where was the mystery in that?

However, if Poe picked a real crime to recreate, one that was still unsolved, he would not be subject to such deliberations. "I have a proposition to make," he wrote to the editor of a Baltimore newspaper, hoping to drum up support for his new story. "A young grisette, one Marie Roget, has been murdered under precisely similar circumstances with Mary Rogers. Thus under pretense of showing how Dupin unraveled the mystery of Marie's assassination, I, in fact, enter into a very rigorous analysis of the *real* tragedy in New York." Poe wrote similar letters to other publications, including his old employer, *Graham's*, hoping to find a buyer. In November of 1842, a year and three months after Mary Rogers' death, "The Mystery of Marie Roget" was published in *Ladies' Companion*, another New York monthly magazine with similar features to *Graham's*, but more inclined to attract a female readership. In hindsight it appears to be an unusual choice, but the editor of the *Companion*, a man named Snowden, had been following the Rogers case, even contributing to the reward money himself. He made Poe an offer, and Poe, desperate to sell, accepted.

Poe's story, however, would not reveal the name of a killer. Instead, it only suggested that although one still lurked in the shadows, through Dupin's expert analysis of the facts, *"The murderer* will be traced." Therefore, nothing was resolved, only reexamined and interpreted by Poe. Had this been a "cop-out," as one modern-day Poe biographer suggests? Poe apparently had no choice. Since he based the clues on facts, naming a name would still have been merely fiction. Poe leaves the reader hanging at the end, just as the real case did, but with an indication that the great C. Auguste Dupin, his fictional detective, was closer than anyone else to unmasking the villain.

Two years after publishing "The Mystery of Marie Roget," Poe would be back in New York, this time with Moses Beach and the *Sun* for a story that would send shockwaves throughout the city. Hoping to regain his footing in the New York papers, Poe fabricated a story detailing a three-day hot air balloon trip across the Atlantic. Since the previous record for any manned balloon flight was only twelve miles, if true this would have been a truly momentous achievement. Its significance was played to the hilt by Poe and Beach, who was in on the ruse. Soon enough, the truth was revealed. "I never witnessed more intense excitement to get the possession of a newspaper," Poe wrote, obviously pleased with the response. But its intent backfired: Poe earned a reputation as not being trustworthy. Beach, however, didn't care. He sold an astonishing 50,000 copies and in a retraction issue claimed that while the story was completely false, it had some merit. "By no means think such a project impossible," the *Sun* shamelessly promoted.

Based on their reputations, it should not be surprising that both Beach and Bennett earn a respective place in the story of the *Lexington* disaster. Bennett was in Philadelphia at the time the wreck occurred and immediately came back to New York to rattle more chains. Since the Panic of 1837, the country was in a major recession. It all started when President Andrew Jackson shut down the major federal lender, Bank of the United States, and moved funds to state banks instead. Jackson thought the move would stabilize the banking industry rather than monopolize it. He was wrong; it just led to more corruption. Eventually banks closed and businesses shuttered. By this time, however, Jackson was no longer in office. His close advisor and former secretary of state Martin Van

Buren became Jackson's successor in 1836. President Van Buren made it worse. Instead of putting the money back in a new national bank, he moved federal funds to an independent treasury, which did nothing to solve the crisis. For this, he was soundly defeated for reelection in 1840 by his old nemesis General William Henry Harrison, a war hero credited with defeating the Shawnee at the Battle of Tippecanoe in 1811. It was a complete role reversal. In 1836, the Democrat Martin Van Buren had easily beaten Harrison, the Whig candidate, by more than a 2-to-1 margin. Four years later, thanks in part to the failing economy and the relentless press, Harrison won in a landslide.

Bennett championed the cause and used the *Herald* not only to influence the election, but also to embarrass those who put their own self-interests first. The sinking of the *Lexington* was a good example. Bennett chastised the ship owners and bank presidents for putting personal gains above the safety of the ship, its crew, and the passengers. The boat was dangerously overloaded with cotton and while the currency on board had nothing to do with the wreck, speed in making large bank transactions was a heightened threat, both on land and water. "His censures induced capitalists to esteem the lives of passengers in public conveyances as superior to all considerations of pelf and profit, so far that greater facilities were provided for escape in cases of disaster," an unidentified author, listed only as "a journalist," wrote in 1855. Contrastingly, Beach, far less critical, was more focused on telling the story than on changing it. His special edition in the *Extra Sun* and the full-page spread, which featured the Currier print, sold a ton.

Thanks to demand and ingenuity, Currier's lithograph business thrived after the *Lexington* disaster. He cleverly picked up on the idea of using newspaper boys and pushcart vendors to sell prints to store owners. In this way, Currier made his money upfront. He sold prints first to the vendors, who then made their own revenue by the number of copies they could peddle. Currier also had the good sense of recognizing the potential of advertising within his prints. In this respect, Currier may have been the first person to introduce the modern-day practice of product placement. Several of his cityscape prints emphasized locations of signs on buildings, such as the Equitable Life Assurance Society in New York City. Whether or not these companies paid for the privilege of having their name or logo on prints that sold thousands is not clear. Currier may have just been doing them a favor. Either way, many of the highlighted companies cleverly distributed the prints like business cards.

In the meantime, Currier was selling so many prints that he struggled to fill the orders. So he hired his brother Charles, whose legacy lay in the invention of a lithographic pencil used to colorize the prints. Charles patented the coloring pencil, and the name Crayola is associated with him. Charles' greatest contribution to the firm, however, was to introduce his brother-in-law to Currier.

His last name was Ives.

7
Our best
recruiting agent

In 1852, James Merritt Ives, a painter and aspiring artist, was looking for a job and steady income to support his family. He turned to Currier for help, but it wasn't his creativity that worked in his favor. Ives was pretty good with numbers, so Currier hired him as a bookkeeper. At first, Ives kept a low profile, literally and physically, as he was "short and plump," quite the opposite to Currier's "tall and spare" frame. Nonetheless, they worked well together. Ives kept the business tallies steady and eventually picked up a pencil to do some drawings. Although his credits are few, one thing was clear: unlike Currier, Ives had a sense for artistry.

Within five years, Currier took Ives on as a partner and the company became known as Currier and Ives. Eventually the prints they produced of snowscapes and wintery wonderlands were used as the covers of fold-out cards handed out during Christmastime to share the joy of the season with family and friends. More than just sleigh rides in the snow, Currier and Ives pictures captured memorable moments, imaginative landscapes, and religious sentiments too. Describing the lively prints, one writer enthused, "They are a pictorial record of one of the most colorful periods in American history."

But was it art? Some critics admonished the works for being simplistic and crudely drawn, but Currier wasn't interested in displaying his work in museums. He produced and sold his pictures cheap, so everyone could frame and hang one in the parlor. The original drawings were on stone, so no one could claim ownership to just one piece. In many instances, the artist's name does not even appear on the prints.

Despite this lack of recognition, Currier still attracted many respected painters. Perhaps it's because he paid them well, or perhaps because they knew their work would be appreciated by thousands. Only a handful of artists were employed directly by Currier; most worked on commission. Their names are not widely recognized but today have historical significance. The English-born Arthur Fitzwilliam Tait was one. Known for his paintings of wildlife and fowl, Tait is considered among the finest of the Currier lot. George Henry Durrie from Connecticut was another. Known as "the snow man," Durrie specialized in winter scenes. Many of his countryside portraits, especially those featuring sleigh rides, were eventually used for Christmas cards. In 1942, nearly 80 years after its creation, Durrie's "Home to Thanksgiving" was considered Currier and Ives' most recognizable print. It features a cozy image of a snow-covered country farm as a man, presumably from the city, is greeted at the front door by his welcoming parents.

Thomas Nast was another Currier and Ives contributor, though since most of his work was celebrated in other publications, his association with the printmakers remains murky. Some of Nast's earliest works date back to the Civil War and are mostly attributed to *Harper's Weekly,* not Currier, although Currier mass reproduced some of his more popular efforts. Nast supported the cause of the Union, so his work was often biting satire against the evils of slavery and the men fighting to save it. But the Southern rebels weren't the only target in his sights. In 1862, his work "Peace" was directed at Northerners who didn't support the cause. Upon viewing the cartoon, President Lincoln called Nast "our best recruiting agent."

Some books on the history of Currier and Ives mention Nast's involvement with the printmakers, though most biographies of Nast do not. One can assume Currier could see the value in his works

Thomas Nast. The Library of Congress, Frazier, photographer [1896].

and made them available to the public even though they were not
works directly commissioned by the firm itself. Currier was not
shy about tackling the important social issues of the day, and Nast
would have been on board. Harry T. Peters, author of *Currier and
Ives: Printmakers to the American People,* writes about the political-
themed drawings that included a balloon-shaped space above the
figure's head for quotes—usually a controversial one. Peters lists
Nast as a contributor to these drawings, but does not get any more
specific. "The main idea," Peters continues, "appears to have been
to inform the people of a political crisis and to make that report
visually." For example, in the 1870s, Nast's biting caricatures of
New York's mayor and Tammany Hall shyster Boss Tweed in
Harper's Weekly were so effective that author Richard Zacks in
his book *Island of Vice* proclaims that Tweed "ranks as the most
famous politician ever felled by a cartoonist."

Abraham Lincoln, the candidate and president, may have been
the most famous person ever skewed by political cartoonists, but
history shows he rose to the occasion. Boss Tweed, on the other
hand, went down hard, but not after first trying to bribe Nast to
stop the offending cartoons by offering Nast $100,000 if he would
"go study art abroad in Europe." Nast played along and asked for
$500,000 instead, but ultimately and politely refused the offer, say-
ing he would rather put bad guys like Tweed "behind bars." The
Nast images appearing in *Harper's Weekly* were as unflattering as
they were damaging, portraying the overstuffed Tweed as a "pear
on toothpicks" and exposing the corruption that unfortunately
didn't end with Tweed's ouster in 1871 and eventual arrest for fraud
two years later. As it turned out, Tweed's Tammany Hall successor,
a man named Richard "Dick" Croker who was accused of killing a
man during a brawl on Election Day, proved to be just as corrupt.

Later in life, Nast would lose a fortune in a bad stock deal run
in part by Ulysses Grant, Jr., son of the former general and president. Grant, Jr.'s shady Wall Street brokerage partner Ferdinand
Ward convinced his close friends to invest in stocks where prof-
its were used only to pay out dividends to earlier investments. On
paper, at least, everyone was rich, but the physical money never
materialized and Nast would never recover financially.

Some 40 years later, in 1920, the same type of get-rich-quick scheme would earn a lasting moniker when an Italian immigrant walked into the office of Boston publicist William H. McMasters, looking for investors to buy international postal coupons and resell them for profit in the United States. Instead of helping, McMasters exposed the fraud and forever immortalized the man and the name: Charles Ponzi.

Nast may have been duped by an early incarnation of the "Ponzi Scheme," but he still achieved the lasting fame to which other artists working exclusively for Currier and Ives would only aspire. For many, just having a job and steady work was akin to a successful career. This was especially true for women artists, who were mostly in the shadows and did not generally work for a living. The exception was Fanny Palmer.

A wife, mother, and full-time Currier employee, Frances "Fanny" Palmer did "remarkable and versatile" work for the printmaker on all subjects. "There seems to have been no task to which she was unwilling to set her hand," Currier and Ives author Harry T. Peters wrote. "The many prints made from her drawings record an astonishing proportion of the American scene."

Palmer came to New York from England with her husband Edward and two children. Edward had no discernable talent other than drinking. He also had no intention of working. The family settled in Brooklyn and soon after, in 1849, Palmer went to work for Currier. She received little credit for her work and even signed her name inconspicuously as F.F. Palmer, ostensibly to disguise herself as a man. "Landscape painting occupied the highest rung within the hierarchy of painting," writes Laura R. Prieto, author of *At Home in the Studio: The Professionalization of Women Artists in America.* "The 'lower orders' among artists were likely to be feminized, and thus women artists could find a greater degree of acceptance." But as Prieto speculates, Fanny never had any intention of succeeding beyond her means. She was a working mother, with a lout for a husband, who had to be the breadwinner of the family as well as making the bread to put on the table.

In 1859, however, there was one less mouth to feed. Drunk as usual, Edward fell down a flight of stairs and broke his neck and never recovered. "That's the best thing he ever did," Ives reportedly told Fanny upon hearing the news of Edward's demise. Palmer became even more prolific after her husband's death, producing more than 100 lithographs on a variety of subjects. Palmer's works are not considered as polished as Nast's or other artists at the time, an objective judgment not based on gender since no one knew the drawings were by a woman. Many female artists were doing work secretively or under the guise of a man. Some did the work and never revealed themselves.

Like Clara Driscoll.

In the late 19th century, Louis Comfort Tiffany was a world-renowned artist of stained glass, which included the popular and quite elaborate Tiffany lamps. Tiffany, a painter by trade, took full credit for his work, but in accepting the commendations that came with his lamps, may have also harbored a hidden artistic truth.

Clara Driscoll was the leader of a group of women working under Tiffany at his studio. Calling themselves quite appropriately the "Tiffany Girls," their job was mostly to prepare materials and select colors for Tiffany's work. Driscoll's role in making the lamps, however, may have been more substantial than Tiffany led others to believe.

In a letter discovered only this century, Driscoll makes a startling revelation regarding Tiffany's famous lamps: "Nearly everything you see around is something that I designed," she wrote. Driscoll, like Palmer, sought no public recognition for her work. The letters were privately written to family members and seemingly tucked away forever. One historian claims that if the secret had leaked out while the lamps were being made, Tiffany would have been ruined. Tiffany died in 1933 at the age of 84. Apparently, he never told a soul. Other than the letters, Driscoll took her secret to the grave as well.

In contrast, Currier liked Palmer, her work ethic, and her drawings of beautiful countryside sceneries and expressive atmospheric landscapes. And while he did not purposely harbor her role as Tiffany apparently did with Driscoll, he did not publicly expose her either. This attitude was similar to another artist at the time, sculptor Lorado Taft.

In 1893, Taft was commissioned to make modeled statues which would dot the "White City," the landscape grounds and gardens of Chicago's World's Columbian Exposition, a large fair that was being held that year to celebrate the 400th anniversary of Columbus' discovery of the New World. Taft, who had already earned a reputation in the city for sculpting portrait busts, was flattered by the offer. He immediately commenced work on several statuaries that would garnish the outside entrance and inside walkway of the Horticultural Building. This, in turn, led to a job as the head of a modeling studio where Taft supervised a team to transform small models into larger-scale productions. Taft was thrilled. Until then, sculptors were only being recognized for doing "death masks" and Civil War monuments. This was a chance to let his artistic vision shine.

Taft's studio, known at the time as an "art sweat shop," was similar to the modeling instruction he offered at the Art Institute of Chicago. Among his students were women whom Taft once said were "young ladies who had nothing better to do." This admonishment was not an uncommon attitude at the time. Women just weren't considered accomplished artists. As the deadline for the Exhibition approached, Taft realized that there were simply not enough artists working in his studio to complete the tasks. Most of the male sculptors under his supervision were busy on other projects. He approached the man who had commissioned him, the renowned Chicago architect Daniel Burnham, and asked if he could use the women under his tutelage to complete the work. Burnham, who had his hands full on many aspects of the Fair's construction, quickly replied, "Employ anyone who would do the work—white rabbits, if they could help out." So Taft did, and the women who worked for him became known among themselves as "the White Rabbits."

Although virtually unknown and often uncredited, many of the women who worked for Taft produced fine works for the Exhibition. This included Janet Scudder. In her book *Modeling My Life,* Scudder relates that she initially lied to Taft about her experience as a model sculptor to get an assistant's job working in the artist's studio. He gave her a chance. "I've got to get it along as soon as

Janet Scudder. The Library of Congress, from the Bain Collection [1910–
1915].

possible," Taft explained. Scudder was just as enthusiastic. "I felt like I had stepped into Paradise," she wrote. "He [Taft] never said he was a little doubtful of my ability to do the work, but his detailed directions rather suggested it." Taft was strict, but fair. After carefully watching Scudder do simple clay and armature work that day, he told her to come back the next morning.

Scudder explains that after the initial work for the Horticulture Building was complete, Taft called all the women assistants together for a meeting. "He had something important to tell us," she recalled. Scudder was worried Taft was closing the shop and that she would be out of work from "the only job I had ever been longing for." Instead, she was in for a surprise. "He began very solemnly," she wrote, and then with a "twinkle in his eye," proceeded to explain his consultation with Burnham and told them they were all hired for a year to finish the enlargements for the White City. "So you might begin right now calling yourself white rabbits," he joked.

"It was a wholesome, happy, stimulating life," Scudder would later recall. "How well I remember that vast hall of iron girders and glass walls and roof. It was like some giant's studio; and surely crowded with giants, as we gradually filled it with those huge figures, which when finished, were hauled away and put into position on the buildings." Scudder says that when the girls received their first month's payment—$150, all in $5 bills—they carpeted the floor with them. "We wanted to see what it felt like to walk on money," she explained. "We were about the happiest white rabbits that ever existed."

Although the works were part of a broader vision, and no single artist—much less the women—were singled out, Scudder's contributions appeared throughout the grounds. One entitled "Justice" was placed in the hall of the Illinois State Building. Eventually it was destroyed by fire when several of the White City buildings, including the state building, went up in flames. Before it was lost, however, Scudder remembers a newspaper reporter approached her and asked for an interview. "My first which I interpreted as meaning I had finally arrived," she wrote. It didn't go well. The reporter explained that he knew nothing about art or sculpture and asked if she could write something down that he could use. Scudder was dumbfounded and a little embarrassed. She wrote a few things down, then changed it, then tore it up, then wrote a few things more down when the reporter suddenly rose from his seat and said, "I ain't got any more time to waste on you," and stormed away in disgust.

In 1896, Scudder left Chicago for Paris, where she studied under Frederick W. MacMonnies, a New Yorker who had created a large fountain at the Fair that Scudder admired. Two years later, she was back in America looking for work. She carved out a good living making small fountains and garden sculptures with child-like fairytales and whimsical themes. She also fought for women's rights, especially for women artists, whom she felt were equal to the task and "should never be judged by a Miss or Mrs. in front of their names."

Unlike Scudder, Fanny Palmer was no world traveler. Due to her responsibilities at home, Palmer rarely ventured outside of New York. "Such lack of mobility would have almost certainly disqualified her from a career as a landscape artist," Prieto wrote. But with Currier, it was different. If it took less than a full day, Palmer would go on location, oftentimes using Currier's private carriage. She would quickly make a sketch of her subject using each side of the paper and two different representations of the same scene, both of which would be used in the final drawing. Currier and Ives artists worked in teams, so Palmer would draw the picture, another might add figures to it, and still others would colorize it.

Currier was in the business of selling prints, not careers. Customers didn't demand great works of art; they wanted simple, yet realistic, keepsakes of places they might never witness for themselves. This was the charm of a Currier and Ives print. While most people could only hear or read about a certain event or location, perhaps even dream about going there someday, Currier brought it all home and in vivid color, too. National tragedies, battle scenes, political cartoons, clipper ships, railways, horse races, sporting events–all were subjects of Currier's artists.

Palmer, it is said, contributed to nearly each and every subject.

She produced more works for Currier than any other artist at the time, yet her name is virtually unknown. By the time she died in 1876 of tuberculous at the age of 64, Palmer's back was so stooped and deformed from long hours of work over a drawing board that she could barely stand.

Fanny Palmer and the other Currier artists were all indirectly influenced by the printmaker's early works. While they were competent artists at the time, their work would likely have never been noticed had it not been for the disaster scenes which led to a surge in demand. Like Currier had done with the *Lexington* print, they worked quickly and produced works which expertly represented the subject they were replicating and nothing more. Today, some of these artists' pieces, with the possible exception of the Nast cartoons, are celebrated only because of their association to Currier and Ives.

8

An artist...
of rare genius

〜✺ Other than the *Lexington,* there is no known association between Nathaniel Currier and Cornelius Vanderbilt. Although Vanderbilt had sold the *Lexington* before the disaster, his name was so aligned with the once-mighty ship that the future tycoon was called on to testify on its behalf at the coroner's inquest. "[I] gave instructions to her commanders never to stop for foul weather–if they could see ahead, they were to go ahead," he said, apparently supporting the decision to steam out that night despite the cold weather and threat of ice. Vanderbilt's statement boldly defends the ship's capacity and strength in any weather. The result, he subtly implied, must have been human error, not a deficiency with the boat itself.

After the *Lexington* burned and long after Currier immortalized it, Vanderbilt's vision for rail travel exceeded his ambitious and shrewd dominance by ship. Now he was trying to cross over a body of water, not navigate it. The future was in laying tracks, building towns, and overcoming obstacles such as rivers. He formed the Niagara River Bridge Company and in 1875 commissioned the construction of a railroad bridge that would link the U.S with Canada in upstate New York. Vanderbilt's desire to cross the river turned out to be a selfish one: He refused to pay fees to cross the bridges of other rail lines, including the one that was already moving train cars between the two countries.

In 1851, German-born immigrant and structural engineer John A. Roebling, also known for introducing wire rope to North America, envisioned a double-decker suspension bridge over the Niagara River with the top for rail travel and the bottom for people and carriages. A pedestrian suspension bridge had already been built over the river in 1848, but the need for a bridge that carried railway travel had so far been deemed too risky. Could a bridge held up by wires support the weight of a locomotive? Although two workers died during a construction accident and a cholera outbreak nearly derailed the project outright, upon completion the bridge was found to be sound and questions about its durability and strength were answered. The lower floor opened to public traffic in 1854. Shortly thereafter, after several load tests, the upper section accommodated the trains.

Roebling would go on to receive more fame and accolades in 1867 for his design of the Brooklyn Bridge, though he didn't live long enough to see it completed. During construction preparations and while taking measurements near a ferry house, Roebling's foot was crushed when it got stuck on one of the pilings as a docking boat hit the rack. "The immediate result of the accident led to the amputation of his toes," the *New York Times* reported. Roebling spent 16 days in the hospital, but could not fight off infection and eventually succumbed to his injuries. His son, Washington, went on to complete his father's vision.

At the time of his death, however, the suspension bridge over the Niagara River was still considered Roebling's greatest achievement. "For the first time in the history of civil engineering over 800 feet of water were covered by a single span and a bridge calculated to sustain almost any weight that could be placed upon it constructed and supported by four wire cables of ten inches in diameter," the *New York Herald* raved in Roebling's lengthy obituary, ending with an admission that Roebling's voice would be a great absence for future civil engineers. "The death of Mr. Roebling must be regarded as a public calamity," the *Herald* confided.

Roebling's bridge was not the first to be built over the Niagara River. That honor goes to engineer Samuel Keefer, whose suspension bridge design opened in 1851, the same year Roebling signed on to the railway bridge project. Keefer's wooden bridge was reinforced with steel and lasted only seven months before a combination of strong winds and rains ripped it off the cliff sides and sent it crashing into the river. Another bridge built by Edward Serrell was in use for four years before heavy wind-swept storms severely damaged but did not break it. Roebling himself oversaw repairs by adding a system of guy-wires for more strength. Then, in the spring of 1864, for reasons attributed to a large ice jam, workmen loosened the guys. When another bout of gale-force winds blew through the cliffs, the weakened bridge went with it.

This was the kind of adversity Vanderbilt faced when he planned to cross the Niagara River with his own rail line, the Michigan Central Railroad. Vanderbilt flat-out refused to pay for the privilege of using Roebling's suspension bridge, the only route into Canada from New York. Instead, he decided to build his own. Just as he did with the construction of steamboats, Vanderbilt wanted it bigger, better—and stronger. He wanted a cantilever bridge.

At the time, a cantilever, or overhanging bridge, was considered sturdier than a suspension bridge. The "cantilever" in the name stood for the long steel beams that supported the structure from the bottom rather than from the top, making the tracks the highest point of the bridge rather than the lowest. Vanderbilt's bridge would not only be sturdier than Roebling's, it would be distinctively different-looking as well. In April of 1883, construction began.

In only nine short months, on December 1, the bridge was completed at a cost of $700,000. Four days later, just before noon on December 5, a train engine pulling a tender and a passenger car were poised to cross the bridge for the first time. Due to a heightened sense of uncertainty, invited reporters chose to watch from the shoreline at first. Then, after the train passed without incident, the reporters boarded another train for a jubilant ride across.

A ceremony was held on December 20, when several locomotives pulling a full load of gravel cars crossed the bridge from opposite

Thomas Moran. The Library of Congress, Napoleon Sarony, photographer [1890-1896].

ends and passed the ultimate weight test. "The extreme horizontal motion of the rocker link applied at the anchorage to allow for expansion and contraction was about an inch," the papers reported. The crowd of 10,000 cheered. The bridge remained in operation for over 40 years.

By this time, Vanderbilt's legacy was also on solid footing. "It is clear that the forces he had helped to put in motion were remaking the economic, political, social, and cultural landscape of the United States," wrote Vanderbilt biographer T.J. Stiles. This enterprising spirit can be found in the bridges he commissioned, including the cantilever over the Niagara River. Unfortunately, he failed to live long enough to see its completion. In 1877, five years before construction started, Vanderbilt died of old age and illness.

The two Niagara River bridges were celebrated achievements at the time. Not only did they tie together neighboring countries, but their significance was heightened by the proximity to one of nature's most beautiful creations, a steep cliff carved out of rock where the river drops like a natural shower continuously falling some 170 feet to an array of jagged rocks and constant spray below. Niagara Falls was the largest and most spectacular natural waterfall anyone had ever seen.

The opportunity to see a natural wonder like Niagara Falls was a privilege to which most Americans were not accustomed. In the early 19th century, only Native Americans and a few explorers and traders had traversed the land between the Mississippi River and California where naturally carved beauties abounded. In time, however, written accounts from early explorations soared with claims of steep gorges, swiftly running rivers, bubbling fountains, and miles upon miles of crags and canyon walls as long as they were deep. The nation was easily fascinated by the stories from these first observers, but it wasn't enough. More than just words on a page were needed to truly appreciate its beauty.

An English-born painter and printer named Thomas Moran is credited with being the first person to capture images of the western landscape, including massive colorful recreations he titled *Chasm of the Colorado River* and *The Grand Canyon of the Yellowstone*. Moran's journey out West can be credited to Jay Cooke, a wealthy railroad magnate. Cooke invited Moran to go on a 40-day expedition he was sponsoring to the uncharted lands of Yellowstone. Cooke's team from the Hayden Geological Survey, led by Dr. Ferdinand Hayden himself, was comprised mostly of scientific types: mapmakers, zoologists, botanists, and an ornithologist. Moran was none of these; he was an artist. Hayden had allowed and even encouraged eager artists to tag along before, but in the end had little to show for it. During one of the team's previous expeditions called the Great Western Surveys, a landscape artist named Sanford R. Gifford joined the group in mid-trek but proceeded to accomplish very little. Disappointed with Gifford, Hayden had had it with artists.

But money talks, and Cooke certainly had the money. He presented Moran as "an artist...of rare genius," and left the team with no other choice. Moran would pay his own expenses and only asked that he be given at least six feet of tent space per night. The accommodation proved well worth it. "What he drew and painted that year, and what Ferdinand Hayden found on his expedition," wrote author Simon Winchester in his book *The Men Who United the States*, "would have lasting consequences for America's perception of the glories of her countryside."

The paintings are some of the earliest views of a land that, thanks to the Transcontinental Railroad, people would soon have a chance to experience for themselves. President Abraham Lincoln's vision of joining the Central and Pacific Union railroads was realized in 1869, just a year before Cooke's team set off, so the timing was perfect. Beyond the purple and sun-tinged peaks lay the wonders captured by Moran's brush. Still dangerous to reach even by train across the western plains, Yellowstone was only for the more adventurous types. Of course, many new and brave settlers had already trekked westward by coach and horse, but that was to start a new life in the uncharted territory, not to view the natural beauty. The Oregon Trail lay far from the wonders of the mile-deep sunken

cliffs and natural geysers. Most travelers got through, though disease and choking dust storms made living rough and, in some cases,
fatal. (Despite being considerably longer, the water route to California around the eastern coastline and Panama was still a much
safer alternative.)

But as trains chugged through desert and mountain regions and
armies defended against Indian attacks, the West opened up and
more and more curiosities took hold.

9
Do you know her?

❧ While the Western wonders still seemed unreachable to many, the beauty of Niagara Falls presented a more viable option. For New York City dwellers some 400-plus miles away, it was a mere day's journey by train. Awaiting visitors at the Falls was a place to stay, a park to stroll, and a chance for the more adventurous types to stand as close to the impressive dropping curtain of waters as their courage would allow. Still, for most Americans, the desire to see the Falls in person did not exceed the effort to actually get there. Many had to be convinced this alluring sight was worth the trip. They had read of its power and fury, perhaps even had someone tell them firsthand, but wanted more. They wanted a visual representation.

Artists of all mediums came to attempt to recreate its vastness, hoping to convey on canvas what the eyes had seen in person. Painters would set up easels and stand for hours with brush in one hand, trying to replicate somehow the scene for those who could not see it for themselves. Some of the paintings were ambitiously accurate. Frederic Edwin Church's panoramic masterwork, simply entitled "Niagara," depicts the grand scenery from the stilled top of the falling water rather than the bottom. It is so detailed and lifelike, some say that if you stare at it long enough, the water seems to move.

Another man with the evocative name Godfrey Frankenstein

"The Rail Road Suspension Bridge near Niagara Falls". The Library of
Congress, Charles Parsons, painter, published by Currier and Ives [1856].

made a series of sketches of the Falls from every conceivable angle, then transferred each one to large canvases that stood nearly eight feet tall and combined to an astounding 1,000 feet long. As the large rolls were mechanically unfurled one by one, delighted audiences were treated to an entertaining panorama experience complete with live music and a history lesson from Frankenstein himself. As it took nearly two decades of his professional life to complete, the pricey 50 cents per ticket (the equivalent of $15 today), Frankenstein implied, was a bargain.

But for those who could neither see Niagara Falls in person nor attend Frankenstein's show, the next best, or perhaps *the* best, thing was to own a print of it. One representation, rendered by an artist, would hang in parlors and bedrooms across the nation. Yet though it showed the glorious Falls, they were curiously tucked into the background of the print. In the forefront, the focal point of the picture was instead a manmade marvel, the Roebling Suspension Bridge.

"The Rail Road Suspension Bridge Near Niagara Falls" was the work of Charles Parsons, an Englishman who came to America in 1821. In the picture, Parsons cannily places a trio of spectators perched on a bluff. Two women in their finest hoop skirts and bonnets converse with a gentleman who appears to be leading the spirited conversation. A small dog stands at their feet. Author Harry Peters would later describe the print as just another example of "a pictorial panorama of America's youth that deserves a high place in our Hall of Fame." In essence, he was describing the body of work represented by the firm which produced the print: Currier and Ives.

It was published in 1856, a year after the Roebling Bridge opened, so people were naturally curious to see the double-decker for themselves. Parsons' picture satisfied that curiosity. The print's significance, however, goes beyond a mere image. That same year, a new train depot was built in the town of Clifton on the Canadian side of the Niagara River. The Great Western Railroad, Canada's equivalent to the United States' Transcontinental Railroad, was now linked to the Roebling Bridge's tracks and more specifically to the hotels and establishments that lined the cliffs. Next would come a roundhouse, more room for expansion, and eventual interest from the American side of the Falls. Included in this interest was Cornelius Vanderbilt's vision for a cantilever bridge.

One person whose interest was piqued even before Vanderbilt's bridge was built was a man named George Francis Train, whose life of great triumphs, close calls, self-congratulatory accomplishments, multiple doubters, and multiple admirers will be examined later. In 1850, in Syracuse, New York, as a 21-year-old dynamo, Train was simply waiting at a depot for a train when a striking young girl standing on the platform caught his eye. "Do you know her?" a mate asked. "I never saw her before," Train answered, transfixed, "but she shall be my wife."

Train conveniently took a seat opposite the girl and proceeded to strike up a conversation. An older gentleman introduced himself as Dr. Wallace, and the girl as Miss Davis, the daughter of Colonel George Davis of Louisville, Kentucky, and a former aide to General Winfield Scott in the Mexican War. Wallace was a family friend who was escorting Miss Davis back south to be with her family. Before steaming to Kentucky, however, they were stopping in Oswego, New York, to "see the sights."

"In such matters—for love is like war—quickness of decision is everything," Train later wrote. He immediately changed his plans. Train declared that he too was going in the same direction. "I would have gone in any direction, if only I remained her fellow passenger." Train was scheduled to sail across the Atlantic to England to help manage his uncle's shipping business. Shortly before going abroad, however, he was granted a two-month vacation. "This was my only holiday I had in four years," he declared. Train could have roused her interest by explaining that just prior to their chance meeting he had visited Mount Vernon, Georgetown, West Point, and the White House where, as a representative of the shipping industry, he had a face-to-face with President Zachary Taylor.

This impressive tale might well have been a good conversation starter for Train in his attempt to woo the beautiful stranger. Their destination, however, proved to be just as instrumental in winning over the girl's affections. Lying just east of Rochester, the town of Oswego, New York, is accessible by a scenic journey down the southern coast of Lake Ontario to a more remarkable destination: Niagara Falls. The Falls was already earning a reputation as a place for the lovestruck as well as the lovelorn. Could Train win over the girl's affection by going to the impressive falling waters? That was yet to be determined.

"And so we arrived at Niagara Falls together," he wrote in eager anticipation.

"Niagara Falls", 1857. The Library of Congress, from the Detroit Publishing Co. Collection, Frederic Edwin Church, painter [1900-1912].

Part II

～ Walter Madigan had a short walk to work on August 11, 1887. It was a cloudy night, perhaps a sign of rain, he thought. Madigan was anticipating another long night of mixing and molding a sloppy brew of sand, clay, and lime at the brick and tile factory where he manned the "midnight to morning" shift in Chatsworth, Illinois, not far from the Indiana border. It had been a typically hot summer in the heartland, but unusually dry. The slight breeze Madigan felt was welcoming. A little rain would be even better.

Upon his walk, Madigan's booted feet thudded across his own handiwork. Wood and cobblestone sidewalks were being replaced by laid brick. Churches in need of sturdier brick facades were passing extra collection plates during Sunday services. The plant was busy. Just three years before, a new crusher was brought in to "pulverize the clay, and make it a much better grade," and in 1882 a new drying shed was erected. "The brick machine is in the ground," the papers noted, "and they will be making brick before many days." Only one time since opening in 1879 had the plant shut down operations, in 1881 to mourn the assassination of President Garfield.

Madigan raised his kerosene lantern and walked across the tracks near the town's railroad depot. Perhaps a little late tonight, he thought, but understandable considering the circumstances. The train had come to town, and what a sight it was. Even at such a late hour, the lights flickered in the coaches and singing could be heard from the slightly ajar windows. This was a *Toledo, Peoria & Western* passenger train, and for the townsfolk who bravely waited for its late arrival, the longest one they had ever seen.

Most of the passengers had boarded in Peoria, Illinois, a railroad hub located in the middle of the state and the largest city on the Illinois River. Peoria had just built a new Grand Central Station, where earlier that evening several hundred excited patrons had boarded the passenger cars and settled in for a long but rewarding journey. They were, after all, going to arguably the biggest tourist attraction in the nation.

The stop at Chatsworth was brief. A few dozen passengers waiting on the depot planks boarded with little fanfare. The train was nearly full. Some counted 15 cars pulled by two large steam engines, used for extra power. Others said there could be 20 or more cars. Several late-night spectators watched as the engines puffed steam again and the train clacked its way onward into the darkness.

Now an hour or so later, Madigan carefully strolled over the tracks near the darkened depot. Looking to the east, he noticed something in the distance. Instead of complete darkness, a faint light could be seen. Madigan stopped, rubbed his eyes, and strained to see where it was coming from. It appeared to be moving towards him. If it was the headlight of a train, he would need to get off the tracks, but the light was not bright enough nor coming quickly enough. Plus, it was jumping up and down like a bouncing ball. As the light got closer, Madigan could make out the outline of a person. Now it made sense: the bouncing light was a lantern and the person carrying it was quickly bearing down on him.

Madigan raised his own lantern and squinted to get a better look. When the shadowy figure appeared in his sight, Madigan recognized the uniform of a railroad worker. Madigan asked if something was wrong, but his words were drowned out by the man's shouting. "For heaven's sake, where does the [train station] agent live?" the stranger called out. Madigan had no time to react. The man's next few words made his blood run cold.

"The Niagara excursion is in the ditch several miles east of here," he cried, "and I am afraid it will catch fire before we can get help!"

1

The equivalent of a million bathtubs

ᑔᕏᕲ For one fleeting moment in time, the beauty and grandeur of Niagara Falls was grossly underappreciated. "The most awful scene...that we had ever seen," was one early explorer's initial response to experiencing the Falls in the mid-18th century. The frightful reaction had been preceded by a harrowing journey through a deep forest, broken rocks, and a swift-moving, rapids-filled river. By the time the Falls came into view, the sound and fury were more intimidating than rewarding. But they had been warned—this was not a discovery, but a confirmation.

Formed by rock and ice over millions of years, the Falls began first as slow-moving glaciers that froze, melted, and moved farther and farther south until land washed away and gorges created the swiftly moving rivers and large pools of water that were to become the forerunner of today's Great Lakes. Over time, this process of freezing and melting chipped away the earth until a mighty wall nearly two miles long emerged. When the last incursion finally occurred some 30,000 years ago, a mountain of constantly falling water was left behind.

One of the earliest to witness the Falls was Father Louis Hennepin, a butcher's son from Belgium. While on a mission in 1683 with French explorer René-Robert Cavelier, sieur de La Salle, Hennepin recorded the first description of the fallen waters. Until then, others had heard the power of the spray from miles away and marveled at its mystery. Perhaps some may have ventured close enough to see them, but Hennepin was the first person to jot down his thoughts. Luck played a role too. No mission was undertaken without the accompaniment of a priest, and Hennepin was a priest. So when the King of New France sent Hennepin to Fort Frontenac in 1675, now the current site of Kingston, Canada, his mission work was put on hold to provide La Salle's advance company of 16 men with a little spiritual guidance.

Their journeys landed them in friendly Native North American tribe territory along the swiftly moving rapids of the Niagara River. From that point they were led along a trail to the Falls. There, from a tree-infested vista named Clifton Hill, they witnessed the rush of water as it cascaded down the precipice to the gorge below –200,000 cubic feet of water, in fact, or as one writer surmised, "the equivalent of a million bathtubs."

Here Hennepin's descriptions read more like a horror novel, calling the Falls a "frightful abyss" with a "horrible mass of water" and "a sound more terrible than that of thunder." However, the majestic nature of its massive size was curiously enticing. The flat portion of the river split in two, creating a double Falls, one wider than the other. The prospects of such large amounts of constantly falling water put thoughts in Hennepin's mind far greater than just the land it massed. "I could not conceive, how it came to pass that four great lakes...should empty themselves at this Great Fall, and yet not drown a good part of America," he wrote. Hennepin described making his way to the bottom of the Falls and looking up at an oppressive amount of showering water. He guessed that the natives who had once lived in the vicinity were driven away by the sheer force and noise, so loud that to stay would be "courting deafness."

Hennepin conceded to the Falls' grace, too. "It is the most beautiful and at the same time most Frightful Cascade in the World," he wrote, bemoaning its spectacle while still reeling from the immense size and power. Others would later agree with Hennepin about its beauty, but his intentions seem meant to deter rather than encourage a personal visit. He had few to convince. In fact, for most of the 18th century, the Falls remained as remote as it had been for the countless centuries both before and after its formation.

In 1751, another account emerged which was just as daunting as Hennepin's. "You cannot see it without being quite terrified," the Swedish naturalist and diarist Peter Kalm wrote. Dispelling the myth that the Falls was 500 feet in height, as Hennepin had exaggerated—it was more like 170 feet—Kalm's description remains nonetheless horrific. Birds would succumb to its spray, he wrote, detailing how their delicate wings would get soaked and they would fall helplessly to their deaths. Other land-borne animals like bears and deer who tried to cross the river were found "in parts" at the jagged bottom below. In a report written to Benjamin Franklin, Kalm used a decades-old tale about a couple of Iroquois to warn others of the dangers of the Falls. As the story goes, the two Native American hunters managed to use a rope ladder made from basswood bark to climb down the Falls from Goat Island, where if they stayed they would face certain death by starvation. Once in the water, they intended to swim ashore, but the eddy created by both cataracts forced them to retreat back up to the island. They survived by enlisting others on shore to use poles through the shallower but rock-filled water to reach and rescue them.

The point of the story, Kalm explained, was that although the path carved from the Native Americans' fort to the top of the Falls offered more hunting opportunities, the island between the falling waters was nonetheless off-limits even to the most resourceful of natives. Kalm, who admitted he was "but a poor English man," meaning his English grammar was sketchy at best, wrote Franklin hoping his friend and author would translate and publish his report in the *Virginia Gazette*. Franklin did, but only after painstakingly revising nearly every sentence. The impact of Kalm's message, however, was clear. "If the King of France would give me all of Canada," he wrote, "I yet would not venture to go to the islands and I'm sure, Sir, you would follow my example."

Hennepin, like Kalm, knew that due to the risks involved, no one, certainly not common folk, was likely to view it for themselves. His descriptions then were meant to entice, tease, perhaps even impress upon minds. Hennepin knew that very few had seen the Great Falls up close and only he was writing about it. Apparently he felt that he could stretch the truth. He made the Falls bigger, wider, and more aesthetically impressive, even though it was impressive enough without all the embellishments. When the truth was finally revealed, Hennepin felt the backlash. Soon enough, his connection to the Falls came with a clever but embarrassing attribution: "The Great Falsifier."

By the early 19th century, thanks to several more accounts, drawings, and accurately portrayed paintings, Niagara Falls would become just as popular as Saratoga Springs for the moneyed classes that lived or visited New York State. Although it was still a 300-mile, nine-day trip by carriage from Albany, many made the journey. In their fancy dresses and finest duds, they would begin on a meandering canal boat before reaching Buffalo, then disembark and finish the trip by carriage ride or ferry on the docile part of the river. There they stayed at hotels run by a couple of entrepreneurs named William Forsyth and John Brown, who, like the legend of the Hatfields and McCoys, maintained a neighborly feud which lasted for years. Fortunately, the Forsyth and Brown story didn't turn as violent as the frontier families' legendary dispute, but in its own way was just as contentious.

Forsyth's tale is a curious one. His family came to the Niagara area after the Revolutionary War ended, suggesting a loyalty to the King which the younger Forsyth cemented by fighting for the British alliance in the War of 1812. His military service is sketchy at best. His commanding officer Lieutenant-Colonel Thomas Clark reprimanded Forsyth for being "a man not generally liked," though Clark's comments were made after the war ended and during a legal tangle between the two men.

In 1817, Forsyth purchased a tavern and turned it into a three-story hotel. He began a stage coach service from Buffalo and a rowboat ferry service, both designed to bring paying customers to the front door of his new establishment, the "Pavilion Hotel." The lords and dukes whom Forsyth invited to visit were delighted to see the Falls up close, but weary of its owner. The Duke of Rich-

No. 66—Table Rock and part of Horse Shoe Falls.

"Table Rock and part of Horse Shoe Falls." The Library of Congress, Stereograph Cards Collection, George Stacy, photographer [1860-1865].

mond, a frequent visitor, complained that Forsyth might not be
keeping up with his taxes. Forsyth weathered the storm and built
a covered staircase running from the front door of the hotel to
the foot of the Falls. Here, more adventuresome guests could walk
behind the cascading curtain of water. Another path led to Table
Rock, which protruded outward and whose ledge stood only five
feet from the crest. Only the bravest took the tour, which came
with a warning that no one with "weak nerves" should attempt it.
Forsyth jacked up the room rates and soon word spread that the
Table Rock experience afforded by Forsyth's hotel was an experience worth the expense. "I lost my breath entirely," was one happy
patron's reaction. "Yet, pleasure it is."

In 1826, Forsyth expanded the hotel, but from then on, his troubles escalated. Greed was mostly his downfall. "He didn't want a
piece of the Falls," Niagara historian Pierre Berton writes. "He
wanted it all." This is where Forsyth butted heads with his former commander Clark, who secured ferry rights on the river and
bought into a piece of another hotel that was being built just a short
distance upriver from Forsyth's establishment. The man who ran
the new hotel was the aforementioned John Brown.

Forsyth immediately started a landlocked war with Brown, justi-
fiably claiming he was there first, although he had no legal authority to stop anyone from intruding. Brown countered by accusing
Forsyth of bullying. Words escalated into actions. When Brown
built a wooden path from his hotel door to the riverbank, Forsyth
reportedly ripped it apart in the dead of night. Even worse, one
night, Brown's hotel burned to the ground. Brown rebuilt and filed
a lawsuit against Forsyth, accusing him of setting the blaze. Forsyth countersued. The land dispute went unsettled for years. Then
in 1832, the Government of Upper Canada finally ruled against
Forsyth. This ruined him financially until, surprisingly, he and
Brown patched up their differences. The potential for mutually
sharing in the rewards of a bustling enterprise was the reason why.
As more people came and witnessed the grand falling waters, the
more popular it became. "Why is it so exquisite," one New York
socialite gleefully asked, "to stand for hours drenched in spray,
stunned by the ceaseless roar, trembling from the concussion that

shakes the very rock you cling to, and breathing painfully the moist atmosphere that seems to have less of air than water in it?"

Due in part to the government's reluctance to settle bitter land disputes between profitable business owners, there was an ambitious but ultimately failed attempt to get people to bypass the busy hotels and live in the newly dubbed "City of the Falls." When interest in actually relocating to such a remote area waned, efforts and money spent on the enterprise were dropped. It became abundantly clear that tourism was the best way to proceed. So an array of new hotels, taverns, shops, and even a museum opened on a quarter-mile strip just above Table Rock.

"The Front," as it was called, was in business.

In an attempt to draw in more visitors to "The Front," in the fall of 1827, a quirky stunt was devised by Forsyth and Brown and a tavern owner named Parkhurst Whitney. The plan: buy a condemned wooden steamboat, dress it up like a pirate ship, put scarecrow-like, life-sized stuffed effigies dressed as soldiers and well-known military leaders on its deck, fill it with several real animals, and send it down the Horseshoe Falls to results unknown. It was to be as fanciful as it was outrageous. The only living person on board would be a pilot who would guide the ship to a point where the natural current would do the rest.

"The pilot is preparing a balloon in which he will ascend from off the deck upon the brig's entering the head of the rapid," reported the *Buffalo Emporium* in July of that year. Soon after, the paper corrected the plan. The boat would be towed by a guide line instead, eliminating the need for a driver, and effectively ending the talk of a balloon escape, which seemed preposterous in the first place. "He [the pilot] would be quite as likely to go down as up," the *Emporium* joked in retraction. Still, it was the kind of spectacle that would make P.T. Barnum proud.

But what was the point?

The draw seemed mostly in the mystery. "Should the animals be young and hardy and *possessed of great muscular powers*, and *joining their fate* with that of the Vessel, remain on board till she reaches the waters below, there is a great probability that many of them will have *performed the terrible jaunt, unhurt,*" the posters read. The people came in droves, filling the hotels and lining the cliff tops on a crisp fall day to witness the demolition firsthand. Estimates ranged from 10,000 to 30,000. To their surprise, the animal stock lived up to its promise: two bears, a buffalo, two foxes, a raccoon, an eagle, a dog, and 15 geese were all on board.

With the Stars and Stripes proudly waving off its bow and the Union Jack flag flapping off the stern, an old British frigate originally named the *Detroit* but now renamed the *Michigan* was towed to just above the rapids of the Niagara River and shoved off. It was over quickly. The ship broke in half at first, then spun like a top, ricocheted wildly off the rocks, and broke completely apart. Those who were waiting in boats at the bottom of the Falls likely could not hear the muted groans of disappointment from the cliff tops over the roar of the tumbling waters. From their perspective, there was nothing to see. The *Michigan* never made it to the ledge intact; only parts, bit by tiny bit, fell into the churning abyss. When it was presumed over, most of the animals were missing (perhaps the eagle may have flown off). Only an injured goose and a bear were found. "Respecting the effigies," a reporter wrote sarcastically, "of which there were several, the only one I saw below the falls was Gen. Andrew Jackson, apparently uninjured, throwing his arms about and knocking his legs together in the eddies, the only one of the crew of fancy that escaped unhurt."

But the turnout was enough to proclaim the stunt's disappointing results a rousing success. "The Front" was filled with cash-carrying customers both before the *Michigan's* bungled drop and immediately after. The liquor flowed freely, although it was said they only had enough for half the expected crowd. The merchants sold their wares too, at least before they ran out. "I assure you that I stopped at Forsyth's about 4 P.M. and was unable to obtain even a cracker or glass of water," was one writer's assessment. Even the bear that lived through the harrowing ordeal was caged and put on display as an example of a new "Falls of Niagara" that was not only a spectacle in itself, but an amusement as well.

The possibilities of this new temptation would fulfill all expectations and the years ahead would be immensely popular. This is

where honeymooners went before starting a new life, where painters and photographers tested out the latest techniques, where poets
and dreamers and inventors expressed their thoughts and ideas,
and where ordinary citizens watched in wonder as the intoxicating sights and sounds of the cascading waters melted their worries
away. The Falls was an attraction unlike any other. You had to see
it to believe it. Those who witnessed it bragged about the journey,
the view, and the danger.

2

There's no mistake in Sam Patch

♫ For all its beauty, however, the Falls represented something more to a select group of individuals who were looking for an opportunity rather than a personal experience. To these visionaries and thrill-seekers, the Falls and the hurried rapids that accompanied it were as curious an entity as they were spectacular, the kind of curiosity that made seemingly sane people do extraordinary —albeit crazy—things.

Annie Edson Taylor was one.

On October 24, 1901, Taylor stood next to a barrel just slightly smaller than her five-foot frame. Made from sturdy Kentucky oak that Taylor picked out herself, the barrel weighed 160 pounds, was oiled to repel water, and had 2-inch iron rings bolted on every four inches for more strength. It was sturdy and as leak-proof as a barrel would be storing whiskey. The cooper she enlisted to build it, a man named John Rozenski, initially had reservations after Taylor revealed her plans. "You will be killed and me to help," was his first reaction, but her persistence must have paid off. The barrel was going to go over the Falls, she told him, and she would be in it.

Taylor's aspirations notwithstanding, the Falls meant different things to different people. As carefree and romantic as it was to some, for others, it was a means to an end. "As soon as trouble hits," a park policeman once said after fishing another body out from under the Falls, "they begin to think about the place."

The suicide rate at the Falls was astounding. By 1900, some 1,000 men or women had reportedly killed themselves, mostly by jumping. The story was usually the same. Many were seen leisurely strolling about, enjoying the sights, taking the trolley tours, and soaking in the magnificent views before calmly and methodically leaping to their deaths. Most had left a note behind or had sent a letter to loved ones announcing their intentions. They assumed they might never be found. One man ironically named John Lazarus (spelled differently, but sounding the same) came to the Falls on such a mission.

Upon arriving, Lazarus wrapped up his belongings, including a gold watch, and shipped them all back home to Pennsylvania. As not to look suspicious, he bought a return train ticket for himself, but curiously refused the change. He then took a two-hour hack ride, returned to the train station, left his topcoat sitting on a bench, walked to the suspension bridge off Goat Island, gently climbed over the railing, and hurled himself into the rapids below. Within seconds, he was over the Falls. Unlike his biblical counterpart, however, no one could raise this Lazarus from the dead.

In 1901, when Annie Taylor announced her intentions, she wasn't contemplating suicide, at least not consciously, but she did plan on leaping over the Falls.

Taylor's plan was criticized initially by those who did not wish to see a woman kill herself for such foolishness. "It would be fame or fortune or instant death," she said, fueling speculation and more confusion about her intentions. But death came last on that list. Widowed, desperate, and alone, Taylor felt she had one last chance to cash in. However selfish that may have sounded, Taylor's reasoning fit the ideals supported by the women's rights movement at the time, ideals that women like saloon-smasher and headline-grabber Carrie Nation and her Suffragette counterpart Emily Davison were preaching and displaying on both sides of the Atlantic.

In America, Nation became famous for marching into crowded saloons with a hatchet in one hand and a Bible in the other, calling alcohol "the work of the devil," and destroying anything breakable, including the spirit of patrons who dropped their drinks and ran for the door. Meanwhile, in Great Britain, Davison was also turning heads. She set fires, courted arrest multiple times, and even deliberately fell down a flight of stairs—all of this to draw attention to herself and the cause, which in England was the belief in the undeniable right for a woman to stand beside a man and cast a vote. Tragically, Davison's life ended during the prestigious Epsom Derby in Surrey, England, when she causally stepped onto the track and reached for the reins of a horse owned by King George V. The King's horse was on a solid pace down the stretch and could not stop. When the dust finally settled, Davison lay motionless on the ground. Her worst injury, a fractured skull, proved to be fatal. She died four days later.

Annie Taylor, by comparison, was no advocate, but she was a victim. Forced to rely on a man for support, she felt suddenly alone and helpless upon his death. This was emblematic of the larger point being made by Nation: women were being scorned by men who were drinking away the family paycheck. Nation's own first husband had died from alcoholism, leaving her with a child but no way to support herself. Taylor's story was based more on desperation than addiction, but considering how few rights a woman had then to make it on her own, just as tragic.

Taylor's father died when she was young, but left enough financial resources from a successful flour mill business to support the family and put Annie through college. She met a man, David Taylor. They had a son together who died in infancy; soon afterwards, David died as well. Alone and widowed, Annie traveled and worked odd jobs: first to Bay City, Michigan, to teach dance, then to Mexico, then Texas, then back again to Michigan.

In July of 1901, while sitting in a cramped room at a boarding house in Bay City, Annie read that the great Pan-American Exposition was being held in Buffalo and that tens of thousands were there not only to enjoy the large Fair, but to see the waterfall attraction as well.

In a state of hopelessness, she decided to go to New York and jump over the Falls.

By this point, it is hard to imagine if people were overly shocked by Taylor's pronouncement. Already the great Falls was an attractive lure for daredevils and thrill-seekers alike. In September of 1901, a stuntwoman named Martha Wagenfuhrer jumped into a barrel and rode the Whirlpool Rapids along the gorge of the Niagara River. It was harrowing ride, but worth it. Bruised and seasick, she emerged alive and with a story to tell, and to profit from too, by going on the vaudeville circuit and entertaining curious crowds with details about her fast-moving, death-defying adventure. Wagenfuhrer explained to the audience that she had picked the date of September 6 because that was the day President William McKinley would be visiting the Falls. Indeed, McKinley and his wife Ida, who were honored guests at the Pan-American Exposition in Buffalo, spent that day at the Falls as scheduled, but their trip was cut short when Ida became sick from the late-summer heat. Later on that same day, McKinley returned to Buffalo to prepare for a large reception at the Temple of Music, only to be shot point-blank by a disgruntled anarchist. Miraculously, McKinley survived the shooting and was expected to recover. Six days later, he was dead.

It's hard to believe that anything would be more shocking than the assassination attempt of the president, but the following day, September 7, as headlines blared the news of McKinley's injuries, a motion picture film crew arrived. They were there to document another barrel attempt through the rapids, this time by a burlesque performer named Maud Willard and her Fox Terrier that she brought along for the ride.

In a twist, Willard's barrel would be tracked from behind by Carlisle Graham, an Englishman who had already conquered the rapids in a barrel and survived. This time, Graham would swim through the swirling currents with an inflated ring around his neck and a rope around his body. While the cameras rolled, Willard's barrel got caught in a whirlpool and spun widely. Graham helplessly whizzed by, unable to stop. He completed the swim successfully and mugged for the cameras.

Meanwhile, Willard's barrel continued spinning in the dizzying vortex while rescuers could only watch and hope that it might

Annie Edson Taylor. The Niagara Falls Public Library.

finally whip itself out. They knew an intake hole on the barrel was good for air inside. As long as it wasn't impeded, Willard could breathe. Unfortunately, the dog's survival instincts kicked in. The furry companion kept his snout firmly pressed against the hole, claiming the only air supply, and cutting off any oxygen. The barrel was eventually released from the whirlpool's grip, but by the time rescuers reached Willard, she had already died of suffocation.

Willard's death was just the latest in a string of foolish miscalculations. Years before, the Falls had selected perhaps its most recognized victim, Matthew Webb, a captain in the British merchant army and an expert long-distance swimmer. Webb had become the first man to cross the English Channel, a feat he completed in just over a day. This earned him national hero status at home in England, but his more recent accomplishments were even showier than the channel swim. In a test of underwater endurance, Webb became a human goldfish by spending 60 hours (with oxygen, of course) inside a tank and on display at the Royal Aquarium in London. He also did a popular high-dive act, jumping from a platform into the ocean. All this led to the chance to take on "the angriest bit of water in the world," as Webb described the rapids at Niagara Falls.

Webb knew this would not be swimming, but surviving. "My life will depend upon my muscles and my breath, with little touch of science behind them," he said valiantly. Here was the proposal: Webb would attempt to conquer the roughest and most dangerous part of the rapids just below the Roebling Suspension Bridge by jumping in and getting tossed around by the swirling whirlpool. He would also wear handcuffs, from which he would also escape, before reaching the side unscathed. Webb figured it might take three hours to get out of the twisting pool and possibly a few more just to find a spot to slow down and land on shore.

On July 24, 1883, at 4:15 in the afternoon, Webb put his feet in the water and swam easily downstream to the bridge, passed under it, then hit the furious waters. A few times he was seen skimming the tops of the waves, like a dolphin, and then nothing. No sightings, no Webb. Four days later, his lifeless body was discovered several miles downriver. He had a gash on his forehead, suggesting a rock may have knocked him unconscious, but an autopsy determined that a wave had struck him so hard it rendered him motionless. He lost consciousness and never recovered.

The *Saturday Review* of London described Webb's death as a "common scandal," referring to the circus-like atmosphere surrounding the Falls and the desire for some, including their national swimming hero, to come to the tourist attraction and put on a good show. "...A vulgar love of shows and emotions," the *Review* called it.

With that dubious history preceding her, Taylor's barrel jump idea certainly created a buzz. The attitudes and opinions about the stunt were also met with skepticism and fear. It was one thing to witness the absurdity of another human being attempting to drop off the spectacular Falls in a barrel; it was another thing to watch her die.

The curiosity was in the suspense, and Taylor knew it. No one had any idea what would happen to her. Besides the few attempts at circumventing the rapids that led to the Falls, no one had been crazy enough to actually go over it—at least not with the intention of talking about it later. The closest comparison was a man named Sam Patch, a 23-year-old mill hand from New Jersey who had perfected the art of jumping and diving into mill ponds as a teen before taking his act public.

Known as the "Jersey Jumper," Patch delighted audiences by successfully diving off high cliffs and into more populated and scenic locales like Passaic Falls in Paterson, New Jersey. In October of 1829, only two years after the steamboat *Michigan* was sent over the edge, a group of local businessmen looking to cash in on the Niagara promotions reached out to Patch, who agreed to jump into the Falls.

When he arrived, Patch made a self-promoting leap of 80 feet or more just as a primer to "convince those that remained to see me, with what safety and ease, I could descend, and that I was the true Sam Patch," he announced. With that, a platform was built between the two Falls off Goat Island. It reached only halfway up the face side, but still stood just under 100 feet high. Patch climbed the ladder to deafening cheers. He stopped at the top just long enough to take a handkerchief from his neck and tie it around his waist. He kissed the American flag that waved nearby, lifted his toes, and took a long deep breath. Then, with his two hands pointing like an arrow tip in front of him, Patch propelled himself outward then straight down to a target of churning water below.

For a brief few moments, Patch was lost, swallowed up by a torrent like a swirling drain. The crowd anxiously waited. Soon enough, Patch's head emerged. The crowd sighed in relief, then let out a big cheer. Patch was very much alive! He swam to the shore and leapt into the arms of the first unsuspecting spectator he could find. "There's no mistake in Sam Patch," he told the man in a singsong voice. "There's no mistake in Sam Patch." It was great theater and Patch knew it. He quickly arranged another spectacular leap, this time from the High Falls of the Genesee River in Rochester, New York, the state's third-largest city. Patch knew he could draw a good crowd there. Plus, the crowds would be closer to the action, a bonus for a showman like Patch who could ramp up the theatrics as well.

The *Rochester Daily Advertiser and Telegraph* played along, promising readers that "no mistake" could occur during the jump and asking spectators to bring cash donations to help with Patch's travel expenses. The paper also announced Patch's "newly acquired" pet bear would also be making the leap. At the scheduled plunge time, promptly 2 P.M. on Friday, November 6, Patch and the bear appeared. The approximately 3,000 people lining the banks let out a roar. Without hesitation, Patch took the bear by the collar and pushed the animal over the Falls. A few seconds passed before the bear's head popped above the turbulent waters. Knowing the bear was safe, Patch took his position on the edge of the platform. Then Patch, with his kerchief sash, bowed, posed briefly, and leapt over the cataract. It was over quickly. "His head bobbed up several times downstream and scorning a small boat ready to take him aboard, swam and waded to the shore—again a hero," the *Daily Advertiser* described. The crowd was ecstatic, but Patch was not. When the financial tallies were counted, the cash donations were far from what he expected. So he decided to do it again from the same Genesee River Falls at the same spot.

At 2 P.M. on Friday, November 13, exactly one week after his previous leap, Patch stood on the platform again, only this time it was noticeably higher. Patch had the event organizers raise the stand 25 feet, making the actual leap 125 feet in length, even higher than his jump into the Niagara River. Something else, however, was even more noticeable on that day: Patch didn't seem quite his usual confident self. Some say he swayed a bit when he walked, leading to rumors that he had been drinking. Perhaps he had a shot of brandy to keep the chill away, many surmised. Others claim he was clearly drunk. Nevertheless, Patch managed to deliver a speech which was as epic as it was ridiculous. "Napoleon was a great man and a great general," he said. "He conquered armies and he conquered nations, but he couldn't jump the Genesee Falls." While Patch spoke, the crowd of an estimated "5,000 to 7,000," larger than his first jump, anxiously waited.

After the brief speech, Patch leapt. Instantly, it looked different. Patch appeared to lose his form. He spread his legs outward and extended his arms wildly before striking the water. "Such a shocking result had a strong effect on the immense crowd," the *Daily Advertiser* reported. Patch never reappeared. "After waiting in breathless anxiety the multitude dispersed with feelings which can be better imagined than described." The search for Patch was futile. The river soon froze over and all reasonable hope of finding him before spring was lost.

But the spirit of the incomparable Sam Patch wouldn't go away. Some believed Patch was still alive; that it was all just a trick. Then something appeared that seemed to validate the sentiment that Patch had somehow duped them all. Less than a week after Patch's disappearance, the *New York Evening Post* published a letter that was signed SAM PATCH. "Some things can be done better than others," the letter began ominously. "There's no mistake in Sam Patch." The writer goes on to describe how the jump itself was "a hoax," and the death staged. "You must know though," the writer boasts, "that I have performed my last leap by proxy." According to the letter, the person who went into the water that day was only an effigy of Patch, a dummy made of straw and wool. Stones were placed in the stuffing to give it weight. "I was a bit afraid that the mock man would rise," the letter reveals, "but when the mob began to say 'Sam's Dead–he's made his last jump–poor fellow!' given to the gravity as I am, it was more that I could do to contain myself."

The biggest hoax, however, was the letter itself. Patch's body was found the following March by a farmer breaking ice in Charlotte, a Rochester neighborhood on the western bank of the river. The corpse was identified by the black silk sash still tied around his midriff.

Although Sam Patch's successful leap from Goat Island was celebrated and posthumously honored by tour guides who pointed out the very spot the "Jersey Jumper" went over Niagara Falls, Taylor had no intention of becoming another macabre statistic. Since no one had attempted anything so radical before, Taylor hired someone who, believe it or not, had sent barrels over the Canadian side of the Falls, also known as the Horseshoe Falls.

Fred Truesdale was an expert riverman who claimed other daredevil-seekers like Taylor had commissioned him to perform the barrel stunt with animals first. He had done so with mixed results. The collapsed barrel would be recovered, but no one was quite sure whether the animals, who were missing, had actually survived. Since there was no hard evidence either way, none of the prospective leapers followed through with actually performing the feat themselves. Taylor was made of sterner stuff. She had a barrel ready called the *Queen of the Mist,* and a desire to match her ambitions. On October 18, just days before she was scheduled to jump, with help from Truesdale, Taylor had the stunt tested. Inside Taylor's specially built *Queen of the Mist,* Truesdale placed a domestic cat and sent it down the rushing water. The trial run was designed to test the barrel's sturdiness and see if it would break to pieces on impact. The cat was used, of course, to see if any living thing could survive.

The barrel was set in motion and down the Falls went the unfortunate cat. A small gathering waited on shore, including Carlisle Graham, the rapids-defying swimmer, and another daredevil swimmer named Captain Bill Johnson. On the Fourth of July of that same year, Johnson had thrilled crowds by jumping from the sightseeing boat *Maid of the Mist* with a rope attached to his waist. The barrel's run through the rapids and descent down the Falls was over quickly. More agonizing was the wait. After several minutes had passed with no sign of the barrel, the crowd assumed that the cat had perished. Not so fast, it seemed. According to numerous accounts, the barrel suddenly appeared and inside was the cat, apparently alive. The feline supposedly had a cut on its head from being thrown about, but was otherwise fine.

Not all were convinced, however. Nothing but conjecture filled the pages of several local newspapers, including the *Express* out of Buffalo and the *Peoples Press* in Port Welland, which both reported that the cat had no air hole and therefore suffocated. Some reports even claimed that Taylor had sent her own personal pet down the Falls, which seems even more unlikely. Regardless of the fate of the cat, the barrel performed admirably. If this was the only reason Taylor was looking for justification in making the leap, it worked. On October 20, a Sunday, the scheduled date of the leap, the crowd gathered. Taylor, however, never showed up. A few confounding excuses were expressed, but it was clear the jump would be delayed.

For the next several days, strong winds swept across the gorge. Taylor waited while the skeptical press suggested it was all "a gigantic hoax." Then, on the following Thursday, October 24, she emerged. Wearing a long black skirt and large brimmed hat, the widowed woman from Michigan climbed into the *Queen of the Mist* and finally jumped as promised.

And she lived to tell about it.

3
Why, we could have made thousands

When rescuers reached the barrel below the Falls, Annie Taylor was still inside, awake and rattled but otherwise fine. She had a gash upon her forehead along with a few bruises, but that was all. "The doctors in attendance upon her said, that, though she was somewhat hysterical, her condition is not at all serious," the papers reported.

Physically Taylor may have been intact, but emotionally she was not. Almost immediately after being pulled from the water and laid upon a cot set up for her on the American side of the Falls, Taylor's attitude about the jump changed dramatically. Suddenly the first person to leap over Niagara Falls in a barrel was preaching against others from copying it. "If it was with my dying breath," she told the press, "I would caution anyone against attempting the feat.

"I would sooner walk up to the mouth of a cannon knowing it was going to blow me to pieces than make another trip over the Falls," Taylor expounded, claiming she had prayed during the entire trip except for "the few moments of unconsciousness during the descent." Perhaps the caution was also part of her calculated plan. "I'm not sorry I did it if it will help me financially," she added, confusing the point. Many questioned her sincerity, but most felt she was just being honest. After all, only Taylor knew what it was like to be inside that barrel during the 18-or-so-minute ride along the upper river and over the Falls. If anyone was going to discourage others from trying, she had certainly earned that right.

Of course, some things worked in her favor, like the anvil which was attached to the bottom of the barrel and used for gravitational weight. "Had it turned over," one writer graphically speculated, "Taylor's head would have been crushed and her neck broken." As for more details from the victim herself, Taylor was less forthcoming. That, she graciously implied, would have to wait for the speaking tour and the book.

Taylor's book *Over The Falls,* published in 1902, was a mostly straightforward retelling of her adventure. It starts as she rips the currents before the drop:

> I could feel the barrel toss, and often turning partly over, until I come to the first drop over the reef, when the bottom caught for a moment. The barrel swerved, and for a moment, I thought I would go head first, but with a jerk it loosened, turned foot downward, and plunged to the bottom. I felt water close over my head, but was not hurt. The barrel rose to the surface instantly and pursued its course.

Taylor must have felt some reassurance that the slight drop in the reef was a sign that the barrel was secure:

> Again the barrel swerved to the left, and I knew instinctively that it should pursue its course it would be dashed to atoms on the giant rocks near the Canadian shore, but God was good.

At the Falls' edge, Taylor's descriptions become more candid:

> As I reached the brink the barrel did what I thought it would do, paused for a moment and then made the awful plunge. The feeling was of absolute horror, but I still knew when I struck the lower river. The shock was not so great, but I went down, down until the momentum was spent. Below the surface all was still. Not a sound reached me. Slowly I arose but unfortunately upon coming to the surface I came under the falling water and was carried back of the sheet under the precipice. It was then that I began to suffer.

The coverage Taylor received after her jump was mixed at best.

Annie Taylor's rescue after trip over Niagara Falls. The Library of Congress, Stereograph Cards Collection, Martin H. Zahner, photographer [1901].

Though the local newspapers were kind to her, calling the barrel stunt "the climax of Niagara wonders," and Taylor "a woman of indomitable resolve," the New York press was mostly uninterested. In fact, they nearly missed reporting on it because for one, they didn't think she would do it, and for another, they had a reputation of not giving the so-called "Niagara Cranks" a stitch of space.

Taylor's hope that her miraculous leap would explode off the pages like a rocket was diffused by an indifferent and some might say inconsiderate press. She returned home to Bay City, Michigan, to a hero's welcome, was paid for a few store window appearances in larger cities like Detroit and Cleveland, and then went mostly away to rest.

Taylor's last chance to make any significant financial gain from the leap was to display the barrel and exploit a black cat, said to be her own and advertised as the same one that preceded her in going down the Falls. She reluctantly did a few appearances, but her money-making opportunities were already dwindling. Although she had told others that fame and fortune were what she ultimately desired, when asked to appear at Huber's Museum in New York, known as a "Dime Museum" for its cheap displays, Annie politely declined, saying it was not for her. A $500 appearance fee was rescinded upon her refusal.

That type of apathy was the final straw for her shifty manager, a man who until this point has remained unmentioned but had been by Taylor's side since she arrived at the Falls. Frank "Tussie" Russell was a two-bit P.T. Barnum copycat who promoted circus acts in Taylor's hometown of Bay City to limited success. When Taylor hired him to promote her barrel jump idea, Russell could see the potential after the stunt, not necessarily the stunt itself. True, Russell helped Taylor arrange the making of the barrel, encouraged the test run with the domestic cat, and even helped her with excuses when the press demanded answers after Taylor failed to show on her original jump date. (Russell blamed her absence that day on publicity photos that had not been developed yet. After all, she needed the money, he explained.)

Russell was more instrumental after Taylor's leap, but just as misguided. Taylor had told him she was much younger than her actual age, although her appearance of a stout, dowdy woman with graying hair suggested otherwise. "She is a widow, 42 years old, intelligent and venturesome," Russell announced on his arrival to Niagara Falls to promote the event. "She had scaled the Alps, made dangerous swimming trips, and explored wild, unknown countries." It was all hogwash. Nevertheless, Russell worked it. Taylor, if she survived the fall, would emerge a star, travel the speaking circuit, and make a pile of dough. Russell all but guaranteed it.

The problem is that Taylor was not 42 as she had claimed, but 63, and never fully recovered from the shock of the fall. Although she wasn't seriously injured, the aches and pains suffered as a result of being battered about in the barrel slowed her down considerably. She dropped nearly 30 pounds and when Russell realized she could not handle the demands of a celebrity, he turned to his own self-interests instead, leaving his association with Taylor with indignation. "If she had been a beautiful girl," Russell reportedly said, "why, we could have made thousands."

Here the story turns scandalous. Taylor claims Russell stole her barrel and sold it to a theater company in Chicago. A fuming Taylor reportedly went to the Windy City, hired a lawyer, and legally took possession of the barrel, which she had found displayed in a department store window. Encouraged and less debilitated by her injuries, she hired a new manager, a man named William A. Banks, and began making appearances at state fairs. But even Banks proved to be less than trustworthy. He, too, sold the barrel for $500, and to this day its whereabouts remain unknown. Though Taylor had a replica made of the barrel and tried to promote it in an odd display at a Niagara Falls restaurant, it failed to attract the kind of attention she hoped.

In one last fleeting attempt to gain the acceptance and notoriety that eluded her, in 1906, Taylor began talking about a second trip over the Falls. This time, she announced, it wasn't to make money, but to give it away. Taylor, the born-again philanthropist, wanted to help others in need, she explained, like homeless women in shelters. Nothing came of it. Broken but not defeated, Taylor lived the rest of her life, as one writer described it, "resolute, proud, a little snobbish, and always optimistic." In April of 1921, residing in an infirmary for the poor, she died at the age of 83. Shortly before her death and still defiant, Taylor stubbornly insisted that she was only 57.

Despite the failure to profit from her exploits, Taylor's firsthand pleas for others not to attempt such a stunt were mostly heeded, but that would change. For one so-called daredevil named Bobby Leach, Taylor's call for restraint proved more of a challenge than a warning.

Leach was a British-born barkeep and a part-time showman and acrobat who performed death-defying feats of strength and endurance to mostly appreciative audiences. In 1907, as legend has it, Leach was a spectator at New York's Madison Square Garden when a man attempted to plunge 125 feet from a platform into a large bucket of water. Leach was envious. When the jumper missed the bucket, Leach supposedly rose to his feet and proclaimed, "I can do that." Whether he attempted that feat is not known, but he did include more dangerous stunts in his own act.

Leach was everything Annie Taylor was not. A hard drinker, he was also a con man and gambler who could spin a good yarn, usually a fictitious one, to anyone who listened. In 1910, he announced his intentions to go over Niagara Falls in a barrel. "The first *man* to try it," the newspapers trumpeted, perhaps finding no other angle to the story than the gender difference. Leach's barrel was different from Taylor's. His would be fortified with armor, like a shield. About nine feet long and three feet wide, it was a barrel in name only. In reality, it looked more like a steel capsule.

On July 25, 1911, the barrel was towed to the site at the top of the Falls and Leach climbed in. The scene from this point is best described by an eyewitness, a man named Walter Arthur, a photographer who was attempting to get actual film footage of the event: "I was stationed on the bank at the bottom of the Falls with my motion picture machine ready and I don't mind saying that I never expected to see Bobby Leach again. Suddenly I saw the black shape of the barrel with its sharp wooden nose pointed on the brink. It hung there for a few seconds before it plunged down one hundred and sixty-eight feet to the river below."

Arthur says the barrel stood up on end for several minutes, as if it were wedged in some rocks, then began to move with the current: "A minute passed, then two minutes, and we searched the smooth black surface where the 'Maid of the Mist' was lying ready to help. Nothing! Three minutes! It seemed like hours, and then a little distance off from the shore we made out the black shape of the barrel."

Leach had fainted during the fall. He was badly banged up, but emerged alive. He was also blindly drunk. The rescuers used stimulants to revive him and then laid him out for a closer look. The news was dire, but not life-threatening. Both kneecaps were shattered and his jaw bone cracked like a walnut. He spent 23 weeks in the hospital recovering. When he was finally released, Leach traveled the circuit, going overseas first where he found acceptance in Europeans who attended his talks, marveled at the dented barrel, and watched in wonderment as the man who jumped the Falls would do smaller—but still dangerous—stunts to appreciative crowds. His return to Niagara Falls was just as successful. He delighted locals with attempts to swim under the rollicking waters and made several parachute jumps out of an airplane over the gorge.

Emboldened by the response, in 1925 Leach announced his attention to jump the Falls again, only this time he had no intention of using a barrel. *Then in what?* he was asked curiously. "Why, in a rubber ball," Leach exclaimed. Leach told reporters that he planned to ride inside a large rubber ball and bounce off the jagged rocks. "This is where I went over the Falls in 1911 and this is where I'll go over again in a rubber ball," he said confidently. Though it all seemed plausible to Leach, others warned him it wouldn't work. So he scrapped the rubber ball idea and retooled his thoughts.

Then in 1926, while traversing the New Zealand countryside by foot, Leach slipped on an orange peel and heard a loud pop. He broke his leg so severely it had to be amputated. Gangrene set in and killed him. "Not a banana peel," one writer aptly jested about Leach's unfortunate and unlucky demise, "the greatest fall artist of all time died from a fall off an—orange peel."

Leach's place in history is perhaps more trifling because he followed Taylor down the Falls. Although Taylor tried to stop others from attempting the feat, that didn't deter Leach. Leach also had the good fortune of cashing in on his popularity, while Taylor did not. Taylor distanced herself from Leach, whom she despised, asking not to be associated with his name "in any way, shape, or manner."

To her last breath, Taylor claimed it was others who cheated her. "Through misfortune and other people's dishonesty," she pleaded, "I lost all of my fortune." For once, there was some truth to her statement. Not the fortune part, that never materialized, but the part about being used for profit by others who exploited her for their own gain. The prime example was the swimmer Carlisle Graham, who was one of the first to reach Taylor after the jump. Graham made a movie about his own accomplishments at the Falls and included Taylor's stunt to boost sales—only it was not Taylor's actual leap that appeared in the film, but a restaged version with an empty barrel going over the edge and an actress playing the part of Taylor.

But Taylor's worst enemy was the person she trusted the most, her hand-picked manager and local show-business hack Frank Russell. Surely, P.T. Barnum would have seen dollar signs in the uniqueness of the event—and not just the gender issue. Russell never questioned Taylor's age. If he had, he might have used it to his advantage. Can you imagine what people would have thought, good or bad, of a 63-year-old woman jumping over the Falls in a barrel?

Bobby Leach was proof that age may have played a factor in his success. He was in his mid-50s and performing death-defying acts, an astounding feat for someone already exceeding the life expectancy of a man born in the latter half of the 19th century. In reality, Taylor was 10 years older than Leach when she jumped, but no one knew it. Russell promoted none of this, instead insisting that Taylor's success would come later when footage of her stunt would play in dime store amusements on coin-operated nickelodeons. But Russell's biggest miss was in not promoting it to the railroads.

Railroad companies were into making money, and the best way to put more people into car seats was to offer more attractive trips at considerably reduced rates. "Excursion" trains, as they were

advertised, usually ran round-trips to big draw events such as base-
ball games, circuses, or political rallies. Longer excursions for a
day or more were even more desirable if the destination was worth
the increased ticket price. Since the bridges and rail lines now
connected many of the nation's larger cities to the popular attraction in upstate New York, people were coming in record numbers.
The rail companies were doing brisk business by offering special
"excursion" trains to Niagara Falls just for the scenery alone. Imagine if a special trip package also included admission to Taylor's
one-of-a-kind spectacle.

One such excursion train is immortalized by tragedy, not pleasure.
It remains one of the worst train wrecks in terms of loss of life in
the history of the United States. On August 10, 1887, just before
dusk, a large train rolled out of Peoria, Illinois. The train was composed of 15 passenger cars and equipped with two locomotives for
more power. Dubbed a "double header," the excursion was a scheduled run between Peoria and Niagara Falls. "The largest and most
successful ever to set out from Peoria for a destination so far away,"
the local papers boasted. "Off for Niagara!"

It never made it out of Illinois.

Shortly before midnight, after a brief stop in the town of
Chatsworth, about 70 miles east of Peoria, the train approached a
small wooden creek bridge that was completely engulfed in flames.
The engineer could see the orange glow of the fire up ahead, but
had no time to stop. He applied the brakes and hoped for the best.
A fireman by his side saw the burning bridge and jumped for his life.
By sheer speed alone, the lead engine made it across the bridge, but
its weight weakened the structure even more. The second engine
wasn't so lucky. The heavy locomotive fell into the shallow abyss,
and one by one, the cars behind it derailed, side-tracked, or tele-
scoped into one another. When every car had stopped moving,
the scene was horrifying. Many had been killed instantly. Others
managed to escape, but were severely injured or maimed. Since it
was the middle of the night, one railroad worker realized the only
way to get help was to pick up a lantern and run down the tracks
towards Chatsworth, the last stop. As he reached the depot, he was

Chatsworth train wreck, Chatsworth, Illinois, August 10, 1887. Kerry Miel-
carek, private collection [1887].

met by a man who was walking to his job at the brick and tile factory in town. "For Heaven's sake, where does the [train station] agent live?" the worker shouted.

Soon enough help arrived, but it was too late to save those mangled in the wreckage. According to one witness, an injured man was so overcome by the carnage surrounding him that he calmly pulled out a revolver from his side pocket and ended his own life. An estimated 80 to 85 people died that night, with scores more injured. Many of the dead were brought back to Peoria by train in ice-cooled freight cars.

The national dispatches reporting the wreck were extensive and thorough. Of note was the size of the train and the destination, which made the disaster even more tragic. In July, just weeks from people boarding the train, an ad appeared in the *Peoria Daily Transcript:* "THE ONLY WAY TO NIAGARA FALLS," it read. "You Can't Afford to Miss It."

"The excursion had been advertised for weeks," relates Louise Stoutemyer, a Chatsworth resident who wrote the definitive book on the wreck published in 1970. "Round trip fare was only $7.50, still, that was a lot for people who were working for wages of two to three dollars per week.

"People did not take annual vacations," Stoutemyer explains. "A trip of this kind was a trip of a lifetime."

Yet despite the awful circumstances surrounding the wreck and massive loss of life, the excursion trains to Niagara Falls did not stop. The wreck seemed to stir the nation's interest in the natural wonder even more. Even the title of Stoutemyer's book, *The Train That Never Arrived,* was as much a statement about where the people were going as it was about how they didn't get there.

It's easy to understand why. Nearly a half-century before the Chatsworth train wreck, in 1842, British writer Charles Dickens embarked on a five-month sightseeing tour of the U.S., mostly by rail. Three months into his trip, on "a miserable, chilly and raw" April day, he visited the Falls. As soon as he stopped off the express from Buffalo, he sensed it: "I saw two white clouds rising up slowly and majestically from the depths of the earth. That was all. At length we alighted; and then for the first time I heard the mighty rush of water, and felt the ground tremble beneath my feet."

Dickens' recollections of the Falls were included in his book *American Notes for General Circulation, 1842,* published that same year. The famed novelist's directive was to observe North American life and report on its progress. His view, however, was influenced by English sensibilities over the Panic of 1839, caused in part by the Bank of England raising interest rates on imported goods, mostly silver, and forcing U.S. banks to do the same. British loans had fueled American expansion, and when lending slowed, the U.S. economy weakened as a result. "I have many friends in America, I feel a grateful interest in the country, I hope and believe it will work out a problem of the highest importance to the whole human race." Heady stuff for sure, and Dickens didn't hold back, especially with his criticisms of the American lifestyle and its unsanitary practices, like the habit of men chewing and spitting tobacco in public. "A copious shower of yellow rain," he wrote in disgust.

A highlight, however, was Niagara Falls, the furthest northern point of his trip. In a rare moment of receptivity, Dickens praised the Falls with his usual flair for poetic prose: "What voices spoke from out the thundering water; what faces, faded from the earth, looked out upon from its gleaming," he wrote. Dickens implied that this was truly the work of a divine power: "What heavenly promise glistened in those angel tears, the drops of many hues, that showered around and twined themselves about the golden arches of which the changing rainbows made! ... Peace of mind, tranquility, calm recollection of the dead, great thoughts of Eternal Rest and Happiness: nothing of gloom or terror."

Dickens' words would echo across the land, as others would as well, evoking God the Creator as the One who bestowed this wonder on the world. Even John Quincy Adams, the sixth president, praised the Falls as "a pledge of God's to mankind that the destruction of these waters shall not again visit the earth." This is why hundreds packed special trains and headed to that place called "Niagara" to see it, touch it, and feel it. Even an English bloke like Dickens thought as much: "...[The Falls] was at once stamped upon my heart, an Image of Beauty; to remain there, ageless and indelible, until it pulses cease to beat, for ever."

By the time Dickens had viewed the Falls "from all points of view," it was assumed that no one could augment its already alluring beauty and lore. Only the birds had seen the Falls from an angle unavailable to the human eye. Yet soon even that obstacle was to be conquered by a man who boldly envisioned a sky filled not just with birds, but people.

4
No great shakes, after all...

CO Ballooning was certainly not a new concept. Its applica-
tions in practical flight date back to the late 18th century when
a French chemist named Dr. Jacques Alexandre César Charles
launched a hydrogen balloon from central Paris that traveled over
20 astonishing miles to the town of Neses. Watching that day was
the U.S. ambassador to France, Benjamin Franklin, who viewed
the spectacle with a telescope from the comfort of his carriage.
"Someone asked me—what's the use of a balloon," Franklin later
explained about the impact of what he had witnessed. "I replied—
what's the use of a new-born baby?" Franklin's wry humor masked
other more calculated thoughts about the future of ballooning. He
warned a friend, Sir Joseph Banks, the famed British naturalist,
that military use of balloons was imminent. Banks' younger sister Sophia had sprightly amassed a large collection of colorful balloon memorabilia, mostly trinkets and drawings, which may have
struck Franklin as more a threat than a hobby.

Franklin's warning notwithstanding, until the mid-19th century, many balloonists focused on advancing the medium in more
practical ways, some in thoughts and others in deeds. In fact, in
France, many scientists and mathematicians took up the cause,
hoping to address an ages-old mathematical and scientific question: *How high can a person go before he passes out from lack of*

oxygen? To achieve such results, any person conducting the experiment would have to stay awake or else risk certain death. Thus, only a close proximity to the actual answer was ever offered. These advances in science particularly intrigued one future balloonist: John Wise, a Pennsylvanian. As wise as Wise was to the prospects of ballooning, he was just as fascinated by the study of the skies, specifically the cosmos, the moon, stars, and shooting comets giving him "rapturous joy."

Good with his hands, Wise had already learned the trade of piano- and cabinet-making, picked up from his father, a carpenter and carver. Soon a boy's love of the stars led to a passion to fly among them. Not only could Wise make a large balloon, but thanks to an early desire to preach, Wise could talk a good game, too. Extolling the virtues of ballooning, Wise made his passion sound important and indispensable. Ballooning was the future of mass travel, he sermonized, and he was just the person to make it happen.

John Wise got to work. He published a book and petitioned Congress for public funding. By using large sums of his own money to stage massive balloon exhibits (one balloon was 120 feet high), he provided glimpses of his vision. This meant nothing to the U.S. government, which would eventually invest millions of federal dollars on railroading, not ballooning. Consequently, Wise gathered up some wealthy friends and in 1853 formed his own company, the Trans-Atlantic Balloon Corporation. Wise believed there was a permanent west-to-east current blowing directly over the American continent and that this super skyway could be used to move people and goods from the Pacific to the Atlantic and then over the Atlantic to Europe. To prove this point, he took to the skies.

Wise assembled a team of two others to join him: a 29-year-old journalist from New York named John LaMountain and an investor, Oliver A. Gager, from Vermont. The hydrogen-filled balloon made of fine silk was, as Wise described it, "a spheroid of fifty-feet in diameter transversally and sixty-feet perpendicularly." Suspended nine feet below the balloon's hoop was a "wicker car" made of hemp and canvas. Below that was a 16-foot lifeboat "capable of carrying in the water a thousand pounds," just in case of wet landings.

While the idea of a 3,000-mile voyage from the Pacific to the Atlantic was the ultimate goal, Wise wisely decided on a shorter but still impressive launch point of St. Louis, Missouri, instead. From there, the airborne crew would follow the Mississippi River to the Illinois River, skirt the bottom of the Great Lakes, reach the Canadian border, and finally arrive somewhere in upstate New York, most likely Rochester. It would be a trip of about 1,000 miles— a feat Wise thought they could pull off in one full day. To add to the drama, an eager reporter from the *St. Louis Republican,* William Hyde, propositioned Wise to take him aboard. "To this we cheerfully assented," Wise said.

Wise also stowed on board a mail bag from the American Express Company filled with "papers from the Pacific coast, and letters from citizens of St. Louis to their friends in the East as a token of their appreciation of the novel mode of mail carriage thus to be inaugurated." The prospect of this profitable venture, Wise realized, would help pay back investors. In practical terms, it would reduce the amount of time a letter took to arrive at its destination from weeks to days. This idea proved prophetic. Before taking his momentous solo flight across the Atlantic Ocean in 1927, Charles Lindbergh was a pilot for the newly established U.S airmail service. Neither Wise nor Lindbergh actually invented the idea of flying the mail by air, but both men helped pioneer it. Wise's exploits even began in St. Louis, home of Lindbergh's base airport for his Midwest mail route and the birthplace of his famous plane, *The Spirit of St. Louis.*

The similarities, however, end there.

On July 1, 1859, the *Atlantic,* Wise, and his crew were off. A launch on July 4th would seem to have been more symbolic, but the anxious Wise apparently couldn't wait. Wise claimed there was a more technical reason for his hastiness. Once a balloon is filled, it should find air, he insisted. Now in flight, Wise was in his glory: "The fruitful fields of Illinois were now passing rapidly underneath us, seemingly bound for a more western empire." Wise estimated they were traveling at 50 miles per hour.

By night, they had reached Indiana and witnessed an impressive starlit Midwestern sky. The air was colder the higher they went, but the westerly winds were cooperating. The four men drank the chill away with brandy and "talked to the dogs," as Wise put it, by calling out in the still night to hear the farm dogs bark in response to their voices. This way they established they were still over land.

The next morning, Wise could see people waving and cheering them on. This struck Wise as odd, since he felt the speed of his flight preceded any communication by ground. *How did anyone know where they were?* He had completely miscalculated. The telegraph lines which ran along the rail routes were transcoding messages quicker than Wise's balloon and the people in New York were already anticipating their arrival.

Before the trip was over, Wise would have one more notable comparison. Like "The Great Falsifier" Father Louis Hennepin before him, Wise would explore Niagara Falls for the first time, and this time from a completely new and unexplored vantage point—two miles above and looking down. As had Hennepin, Wise jotted down his thoughts. These were later transcribed for an epic 800-page book about the flight, which included in its original 10-sentence, 95-word title a biblical quote from Job: "Stand still, and consider the wondrous works of God." The title was later shortened to just the first three words: *Through the Air.* "Do you see what a wonderful cloud manufactory this Niagara is?" Wise marveled, adding poetic-like flourishes to his praise. "Cloud upon cloud is rising up from its evaporized water. See how orderly they take their line of march eastwards, as they rise up, perhaps to carry their treasured moisture to some distant parched land."

Wise's descriptions of "beautiful miniature rainbows" and "faery-like" appearances would only enhance the experience. "And now listen to the music," he continued. "It is not a roaring, thundering, dashing, tumultuous sound, but music of a sweetest cadence." Apparently, Wise's balloon-mates shared differing opinions. Hyde, the journalist, was especially unimpressed. "The famous Falls were quite insignificant, seen from our altitude," he noted. "There was to us, a descent of about two feet, and the water seemed to be perfectly motionless. The spray gave the whole appearance as ice, and there was nothing grand or sublime about it." Hyde snidely compared the spray from the bottle of champagne they uncorked upon arriving as being "livelier" than the grand Falls itself. Gager, who was along for the ride because he helped pay for it, observed that the sight of the cascading falls from high above was "no great shakes, after all." Similarly, LaMountain, the other writer, thought the falling waters looked like a "clever little mill-dam." Undaunted, Wise was not so willing to pass off the view as trivial and inconsequential. He recognized the moment and embraced it. "It is a sublime spectacle this–a laboratory of nature–an irrigating engine," he wrote glowingly. "Nothing is formed in vain."

Shortly after the Falls was left behind, the trip took a turn for the worse. The winds gathered, raged, and changed directions. Wise had to make some quick decisions. The winds were punching the balloon in a northward direction directly towards Lake Ontario, notorious for its tornado-like columns of swirling water. Above it all, the *Atlantic* continued to soar like a bird. "With all the rapid speed of the balloon, and with all the commotion in clouds of dust below, and the miniature performances of the whirlwind on the surface of the earth, in our position, there reigned a dead silence," Wise countered. "The fibre of a cobweb would not have ruffled if suspended in our car or boat at the height we were sailing."

While still flying over solid earth, Wise let out the gas valve. They slowly started to descend, but the ground ended before they could safely land. Lake Ontario now opened up beneath them. Wise suggested they climb into the lifeboat, cut the ropes, and hope for the best. But LaMountain had a better idea: Cut the heavy double-planked bottom of the life boat, the seating, and everything else not needed and leave just the canvas shell. This way, they could reduce the weight but still use the boat if necessary. Perhaps the lighter balloon would float just high enough above the water until help arrived or land reappeared. It took some effort and LaMountain was nearly swept away when the boat scraped the waves, but he managed to make the adjustments and climb back in the basket, losing only his hat in the process. Looking from above, Wise could see only the hat floating helplessly away "LaMountain's gone," he shouted. "No, I ain't," LaMountain shouted back.

Mostly everything else on board went over the side too, including the instruments, cigar cases, the champagne and brandy bottles,

John Wise balloon flight descent, July 1859. The Library of Congress, *Frank Leslie's Illustrated Newspaper* [July 16, 1859].

and lastly the mail bag. For now, the plan was working. The balloon rose slightly, but still the prospects of a rough landing was imminent. "The chance between drowning and that of being mincemeat among the rocks and trees was enough to appall the hearts of strong men," Wise recounted. Then hope. A steamer named the *Young America* cutting through the rough waters spotted the wayward balloon in distress. Wise thought they should ditch the balloon and swim to the vessel, but the others told him to wait. "If I was to die," Wise recalls Hyde telling him, "let us die on land if we can reach it." They waved goodbye to the ship's crew, let out "three cheers," and swept past.

After two-and-a-half hours, they finally reached the shores of Henderson Township, New York, near the Canadian border. The balloon, still traveling at an estimated 60 miles an hour, crash-landed in a grove of trees. Wise thought they were surely doomed, but the huge elm branches shredded the balloon's skin and slowed down the momentum. When the basket finally stopped, the four occupants were left hanging by the ropes 50 feet above ground, but all very much alive and, even more surprisingly, uninjured. Wise wrote later that a small crowd soon gathered and an elderly woman stepped forward, looked up over her spectacles, and asked where they came from. "St. Louis," was the response from above.

"How far is that from here?" she inquired.

"About a thousand miles," Wise answered back.

Wise claimed victory. The trip proved his theory that a west-to-east current existed, and the 19-hour trip was quicker than anyone had ever traveled that great distance before. He defiantly compared ballooning to Antarctic expeditions, institutions of learning, the invention of the telescope, gas-lighting, ocean steamers, and Morse's telegraph wire as examples of thoughts and ideas that many had scoffed would never last. The loss of the coveted mail bag, though, ruined any chance Wise had of developing an idea that could potentially make him rich.

Like Annie Taylor, Wise had his share of close associates who turned against him. These included William Hyde, the journalist, who wrote articles accusing Wise of incompetence and indecision during the cross-country flight. He painted the balloonist as a coward and claimed only he (Hyde) could successfully cross the Atlantic in a balloon, a feat he never actually attempted. He also challenged Wise to a 3,000-mile race across the continent, which also never occurred.

Returning to St. Louis, Wise continued to push the airmail concept and never wavered in his insistence that balloons were the best way to travel long distances. During the Civil War, he unsuccessfully made a bid to use tethered balloons as observation lookouts, a position appointed by President Lincoln which ultimately went to another balloonist named Thaddeus Lowe. Tragically, in 1879, at the age of 71, on a balloon flight that originated in East St. Louis, Wise and another passenger named George Burr, a bank teller from St. Louis, were spotted just west of Chicago drifting toward Lake Michigan. The balloon named *Pathfinder,* which was moving at a rapid rate of speed, soon disappeared from sight and was never seen again. Several weeks later, after acquaintances of Wise insisted the pair had made it safely to Michigan and were surviving–somewhere–by eating berries, Burr's body, presumed drowned, washed ashore. Although Wise likely suffered the same fate, his remains were never recovered.

Poor John Wise. Like so many thrill-seekers before him, the connection to Niagara Falls should have been the biggest and proudest accomplishment of his life–and perhaps the easiest to exploit–but he passed it off as mere spectacle. "[Niagara Falls] was already a powerful symbolic presence in the British as well as American psyche," wrote author Richard Holmes in his book *Falling Upwards.* "For John Wise and his crew, flying over it [the Falls], the first human beings to ever do so, it should have been a moment of national epiphany." Yet, Wise never used it to his advantage. During the flight, he jotted down a few notes in a logbook, including his thoughts over the Falls, but they didn't appear in book form for another 15 years. A series of detailed wooden engravings were made of Wise's descriptions, but not much else.

Granted, Wise had bigger aspirations than being the first man to view the Falls from the sky, and the speed of the balloon's travel would have made the actual flight over the cascading waters in mere minutes time, if not seconds. This would hardly have given anyone on the ground a chance to strain their eyes upward and see the balloon pass. And on top of that, the flight's harrowing conclusion was far more dramatic. Still, considering the attitude towards the Falls at the time, it would seem that an opportunity to cash in was obtainable.

Years later, Annie Taylor would be the first person to jump over the Falls in a barrel, and while her broadened vision of becoming sustainably wealthy failed, she still claimed victory. Sam Patch, Bobby Leach, and others also found their chances for success at the Falls and seized upon them. Even Father Hennepin, despite his frightening overestimations, still gets credit for being the first to describe the mighty falling waters.

History records as many near-misses as successes, and while Wise's story falls directly into the former category, another man's incredible journey paints a completely different picture.

George Francis Train.

When we last left his story, Train was an upstart 21-year-old about to sail to England to manage a relative's shipping business. In Syracuse, New York, his plans got sidetracked. While standing on a platform waiting for a train, his eyes fixated on a young lady in the crowd. Train struck up a conversation with the girl and immediately changed his plans. Now together they would steam to Rochester and from there travel by boat to Niagara Falls, a destination well-suited for a man trying to woo a beautiful stranger.

At this point, Train's incredible life journey was just beginning. It deserves some explanation.

Even the abridged version is remarkable: Train would become America's first foreign correspondent to Australia. He would convince the Queen of Spain to finance the Atlantic and Great Western Railway. He would be accused of being a spy, be thrown in prison numerous times, and be charged with manslaughter. Back in America, Train would go on tour with Susan B. Anthony and give speeches on behalf of the women's suffrage movement. He would enter politics, support the Union side of the Civil War, and twice run for president of the United States. "When his campaign for the presidency fizzled," wrote self-proclaimed Train enthusiast and author Allen Foster, "he ran for the imaginary office of Dictator [of the United States]."

Throw in his being a man of innumerable ideas: "I have from time to time, suggested a large number of little improvements, mechanical or other devices, for which I have never taken out patents, or received a cent of profit in any way," Train proclaimed. These patents are *truly* attributed to others, like the rubber eraser placement at the end of pencil and the "milk pitcher-like" nose of an ink bottle. Train insists these were ideas he envisioned first and just passed along. Train even circumnavigated the globe three times, breaking the existing record on the third try. But that's not all. His assistance in building the transcontinental railroad arguably gives him credit for sharing the creation of America's first major corporation, and in retrospect, a contribution to the corruption that followed. All these accomplishments, embellished or not, would come in due time. In 1850, however, as a young man, Train was simply trying to impress a girl.

Allowed to escort his "charge" about the Falls, Train took advantage of the romantic setting to court her: "I was foolish enough to do several risky things, in a sort of half-conscious desire to appear brave—the last infirmity of the mind of a lover. I went under the Falls and clambered about in all sorts of dangerous places, in an intoxication of love.

"We were at the Falls forty-eight hours, and before we left we were betrothed," Train wrote. "It was the same old story, only with the difference that our love was mutually discovered and confessed amid the roaring accompaniment of the great cataract."

Train's chivalrous dexterity aside, his story of extraordinary achievements in industry and commerce represents a part of the American spirt that was just beginning to blossom in the mid-19th century. Rail lines would soon open up the West. Larger ships, some as long as city blocks, were moving along coastlines and traveling great distances across oceans. Soon, flying machines powered by engines would conquer the same routes. The world was becoming a much smaller place, and Train had his hands in most of these ventures. And then some.

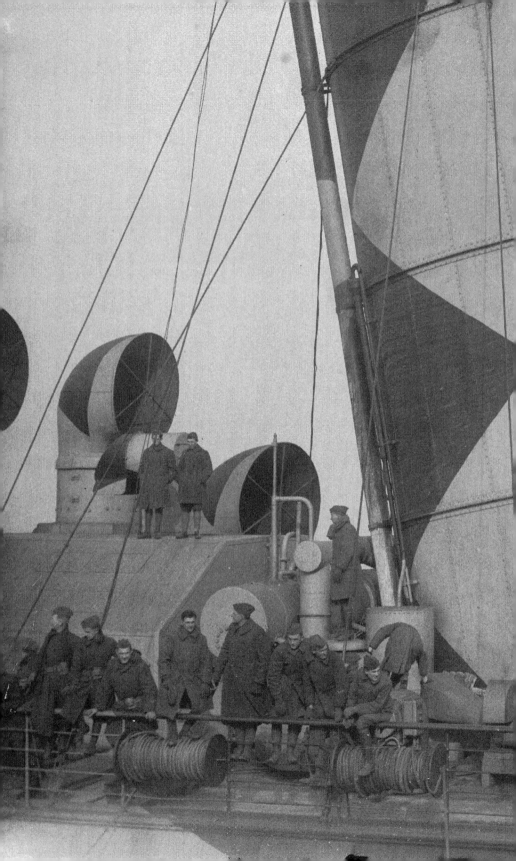

RMS *Mauretania*. The Library of Congress, from the Bain Collection [1918].

Part III

ᗡ On Tuesday, October 11, 1927, five months after Charles Lindbergh made his record-breaking solo flight across the Atlantic, a 23-year-old dental assistant from Lakeland, Florida, stepped into a specially built Stinson "Detroiter" monoplane named *American Girl*. She was attempting to emulate her hero and become the first woman to make a transatlantic flight from New York to Paris.

By this point, the press was already in on the attempt. Ruth Elder was an aspiring actress with an infectious personality and a pretty face to boot. Not shy about her intentions, she told reporters that she had grown up poor in the South and had always dreamed of becoming rich and famous like the unassuming Lindy. "Why not I?" she replied when asked.

Reporters soon followed her every move and pictures of Elder posing next to the plane while wearing a red ribbon in her hair were posted in newspapers across the country. "Ruth Ribbons" became instantly popular.

But could she fly a plane? That she could, she relayed confidently, but not experienced enough to go it alone. So her flight instructor and a more seasoned pilot named George Haldeman would also be on board.

Then, on that crisp October day at New York's Roosevelt Field, the same spot where Lindbergh launched his historic flight, the press huddled en masse to see her off. "Well here goes nothing, that may turn up something," Elder thought to herself as the propeller whirred into action.

Thirty-six hours later, at the Le Bouget airport in Paris, a smattering of journalists and a few well-wishers gathered for the welcoming party. Word had been sent that the plane was just 300 miles and only a few hours from shore. Elder and her companion had already shattered a record by logging some 2,000 miles over a body of water. This was by design. In May, Lindbergh first flew along the New England coastline before heading over the Atlantic. Elder took a more direct route, traveling over the ocean's warmer climate from the beginning of the flight. They also flew around several storms, the press was told.

But the joyous atmosphere soon turned to despair. The hours drifted by without any word of Elder or her plane. The crowd kept looking up, hoping for a sign. Nothing came. Soon enough, the papers blared out the shocking news: Elder's plane was late and her fate unknown.

"Lost at Sea," it read, and "Where is Ruth?" it asked.

The *American Girl* was missing!

1
I will find something to do

ℭ℮℘ By his own admission, George Francis Train was a very important man. He was also quite famous once too, not only for what he did—which, according to Train, was important enough to merit such acclaim—but how he did it, or perhaps more importantly, how he *told you* he did it. "I have never knowingly told a lie; and I shall not at this point of my life," he says in his autobiography, transcribed rather than written at the age of 74, and titled *My Life in Many States and in Foreign Lands*.

The reader is left to decide how much of Train's stories are true. Certainly his travels across continents speak volumes. Train is credited with inspiring the first horse-drawn tramway system in London, and in America a part in the building of the transcontinental railroad. Many towns that popped up along the rail's route owe their existence in part to Train buying land cheap, then selling for a profit once the spikes were laid. Laudable or not, it made him a very wealthy man.

Train was never modest about his achievements. In his own mind, at least, he seems to have sparked, created, destroyed, or debunked about every good intention of the 19th century. Somehow Train manages to be just at the cusp of greatness. His bad timing was impeccable, although blame goes to others for overlooking it. For example, Train implies that if only he had a meeting with Jefferson Davis to express his views, the Civil War would have ended much earlier or perhaps never taken place at all. Apparently, the South just needed some of his sage advice: "I could impress the Southerners with the suggestion that in the event of their abandoning the contest at the stage, they could obtain far better terms than the victorious North could be content to offer after a long and harrowing war."

In a detailed account of Train's life, the aforementioned Allen Foster portrays Train as a veritable saint in the eyes of those who admired him. Foster lets the superlatives fly but doesn't shy away from Train's outlandish behavior. "Few people have lived the kind of rip-roaring adventurous life that 'Citizen Train' (as he liked to be called) did," Foster writes, "the world is a much poorer place for it."

When meeting someone for the first time, rather than shaking the other person's hand, Train would shake hands with his own instead. A custom he picked up in China. In Asian circles, it indicated a sign of respect. In America, however, it was just plain odd. For no apparent reason, Train wrote poetry in alternating lines of red and blue crayon and supposedly walked down the street naked just for effect. When he ran for president—which he did several times—Train charged admission to his campaign rallies. In the *Biographical Review* written in 1888 and featuring dozens of profiles of "prominent men and women of the day," Train is included with the likes of Oscar Wilde, Thomas Edison, and Samuel Clemons. Train's review credits him as "one of the most eccentric men in America," which at the time wasn't a distinction met with as much scrutiny as it was curiosity.

Train was born in Boston, Massachusetts, on March 24, 1829, the same day an unusually late winter-like storm hit the Northeast, dumping 12 to 15 inches of snow. His father Oliver had married a preacher's daughter and moved the family to New Orleans to open a grocery store. Then tragedy struck. Train, as a small boy, watched his family picked away one by one by the deadly yellow fever. First his three sisters fell; then his mother also succumbed to the disease. Only George and his father were left. Train's grandmother, who lived on a farm in Boston, sent a letter: "Send George," she

George Francis Train. The Library of Congress, part of the Brady-Handy
Photograph Collection [1855-1865].

wrote, "before they're all dead." So Oliver put George, only four years old, on a steamship named *Henry* with a note: "Take good care of the Little Fellow, he is the only one left of us in the house, including the servants."

Thus, Train began his first journey.

At the age of 16, George's life would be forever changed by another man, Colonel Enoch Train, his father's brother. Enoch owned a shipping company, and George was looking for work. He went down to his uncle's shipping house on the Wharf and inquired about a job. "I want to make my way in the world," he declared. The colonel told him to come back when he was 17. George came back the next day. "Well, we shall see if we can find something for you to do," his uncle said, surprised.

"I will find something to do," replied George.

For the next decade, George's work in the shipping industry would define him. He was instrumental in producing large sailing vessels that brought goods from New England ports to Great Britain. But while George was thinking bigger, his uncle was not. George suggested that Enoch retain only a controlling interest and let others bring more capital to the business. This way, George explained, they could open shipping houses throughout the world. Enoch, wanting to own and manage his own ships, refused. George knew this was a deal breaker. "It not only put an end to a grand project," George would later recall, "but an end to a business."

In 1853, when plans to expand the shipping business fell through, George kept traveling to China, Hong Kong, and India, often hitching rides on steamers, some of which carried large supplies of opium and were prone to pirate attacks. Train records all this in his book and doesn't hide from the often lurid and disgusting practices he witnessed. These included the slave traders in Macao, China, which he wrote about in great detail for the *New York Herald*, no doubt at the request of its sensationalist publisher, a man not unfamiliar at this point: James Gordon Bennett.

Train returned to New York in July of 1856 and, thanks to Bennett and his correspondence in the *Herald*, became an instant public figure. Bennett hosted a reception in Train's honor and quickly announced, in his typical over-the-top fashion, that Train should run for Congress. Train had no political intentions at that point; he just wanted to return overseas and continue pursuing business interests. First, though, he would go to Boston to be with his wife and daughter, whom he had not seen in three years. Upon his arrival, the joyous reunion was interrupted by several official-looking men waiting at the door. They were there to arrest him. Train was accused of using a credit firm in Australia, making money, but not paying others back their due. It was a convoluted charge that wouldn't stick. Train insisted he never used the firm and had paid up all debts. Enoch helped his nephew post bond, and the matter was eventually dropped. Train would later boast that it was his first "false arrest," adding "from this time for many years I kept getting into jail, for no crime whatsoever."

Train went back across the Atlantic the next year, this time writing reports for *Merchants' Magazine*. The magazine was run by a man named Freeman Hunt, a pioneer in business journalism, who used the moniker "Young American" to introduce Train to his readers. With his family in tow, Train traveled to London, Paris, Rome, and Venice first, before spending a considerable time, nearly eight months, in France. His letters back to Hunt from Europe, Asia, and Australia eventually became a book. By the time it was published, Train had visited places like Java, Singapore, Bengal, Melbourne, and Sydney, among others.

All this was a precursor to Train's greatest adventure in 1870, when he traveled around the world in 80 days. It was a momentous achievement for its time and one for which Train claimed victory, even though there was no precedent or actual record to break. In fact, the scope of the accomplishment wouldn't be truly appreciated until a book came out several years later, giving the feat some substance by championing a fictional character who also completed the remarkable task in the same amount of time.

Train immediately claimed ownership, saying he was the inspiration for Jules Verne's fictional Phileas Fogg from the acclaimed novel *Around the World in Eighty Days*. The source seemed obvious to Train; to others, not so much. Certainly Train's adventure mirrored that of Fogg, especially the number of days he said it took to circumnavigate the globe, but that is where the similarities end. Fogg was a prim and proper Englishman while Train was, among other things, an "erratic and unconventional" Bostonian. Also, Fogg made the journey on a bet while Train just did it on a lark.

Train had some obvious discrepancies to explain, the most glaring being the 80 days assertion. Apparently, Train left out the number of days he wasn't actually moving, specifically, a stint in jail after an unfortunate incident in Marseilles, France, during protests over labor disputes. Thus, the trip took considerably longer than 80 days. Still, Train claimed plagiarism, a charge to which Verne never responded.

Verne, whose novel would turn out to be his biggest success, probably had no idea that a crank from America was claiming ownership of Fogg. Unlike his earlier works, which were mostly written for the stage, *Around the World in Eighty Days* was a novel which eventually became a play. Verne made a fortune on the stage rights before the book became popular. Upon the book's release in 1872, however, Verne was just hoping the story would give readers as much enjoyment as it did him: "You know, I must be a little crazy: I fall for extravagant things my heroes get up to," he wrote shortly before its release. "There's only one thing I regret; not to be able to get up to do those things with them."

Whether Verne knew or cared about Train's self-proclaimed 80-day journey around the world, nearly 20 years later, the famous writer's most enduring protagonist would be in the spotlight again, this time thanks to an ambitious newspaper reporter—a woman no less—who went by the name of Nellie Bly.

2

Look out for me!

🖎 Nellie Bly was a writer, like Verne, but unlike the English novelist's rise to fame, Bly's road to familiarity would be considerably more onerous. Born in 1864 in a small Pennsylvania hamlet on land owned by her father, Bly was given the name Elizabeth Jane Cochrane. Her nickname, however, was "Pink," thanks to her mother Mary Jane's penchant for having her daughter wear shockingly vivid dresses, always pink, which stood out among the drab colors the other children wore. Later, in an article she wrote as an adult, Pink would provide a slight glimpse into her own childhood. In it, she told the tale of a 12-year-old boy, eight years her junior, who wrote her "misspelled" love letters through the "crevices in the back fence." The letters spurred her interest in writing.

Her story growing up in tiny Apollo, Pennsylvania, was also told to readers by a newspaper for which she later worked, New York's *The World*. Bly was an insatiable reader and daydreamer as a youth, *The World* described, filling her mind with fanciful stories she would write on scraps of paper. So alarming was this condition, *The World* noted, "she had to be placed under the care of a physician." More accounts of Pink's childhood from other, perhaps more reliable sources, paint the young girl as a rebel with a cause. Her "riotous conduct" in school got more notice than her "profound scholarship," one description read.

In 1880, at the age of 16, Pink moved to Pittsburgh, where she would begin her career as a journalist. Her father died when Pink was young and although he was wealthy from a successful grain mill business in town, he left no will. The family was left with the house, a few personal belongings, and not much else. Mary Jane sold the property and moved on, eventually getting remarried to a man who occasionally beat her and threatened her life. Pink went away to boarding school but didn't stay. When her brother Albert left for Pittsburgh, her mother followed, and soon Pink joined them in the bustle of the big city. It was a dramatic change for a teenager from a small town. The industry that fueled Pittsburgh choked the city with grim, sulfur-smelling air and ever-present black soot which clung to clothes like snowflakes did to the ground. Still, the grit and grime of the big city didn't bother Pink as much as the prevalent attitude among men in regard to women. After seeing a column written by a man that devalued a woman's role in society, Pink responded by writing a letter to the editor of the *Pittsburg Dispatch.* "A woman's sphere," the male writer so bluntly put it, "is defined and located by a single word—home." Not so, Pink wrote back. She signed it "Lonely Orphan Girl," though she was neither lonely nor an orphan.

The managing editor at the *Dispatch,* George Madden, read the letter but refused to publish it. Instead, he asked the girl to come to the newspaper office. When she did, she was offered a chance to write her own article instead, on the same subject and with the same zeal as her original letter. Soon enough, Pink was offered a job. Before her next article, however, Madden assigned her a catchy name from a fictional character in a Stephen Foster folk song that Madden reportedly had stuck in his head: Nelly Bly. The misspelling of Foster's Nelly to Nellie was a typist's mistake that was never corrected.

In the late 19th century, only two percent of journalists in America were female, and those few worked from home. The newsroom, like many other places frequented by men, was considered no place for a lady. Even if the gender barrier was broken, sexual advances and sneers were usually in order. Most women chose to avoid confrontation rather than fight it, either out of fear or lack of means of retribution. Despite this mindset, the women who were able to crack men's inner sanctum and endure the boisterous behavior and salty language proved they were outstanding journalists.

Nellie Bly was one.

Though her hiring at the *Dispatch* may have been a bit of a novelty, Bly never let it slow her down. She continued to stoke the establishment by tackling the tough and controversial issues of the day. In just her first few months working for the paper, she wrote an article on divorce—from a woman's perspective, of course—titled "Mad Marriages," and produced a popular eight-part series on conditions faced by women who work in factories. Later, looking to escape the doldrums of the newsroom, she asked to do some traveling and convinced her boss to send her to Mexico as the paper's chief correspondent. It was a prime assignment, dreamed up by Bly: she was to report from a foreign land the cultural differences between the two countries. Nellie proved that as a woman writing for an American newspaper, she was not only a crack reporter but a hard-hitting journalist to boot.

When she returned from Mexico, Bly was disappointed that the stories assigned to her were rather less than biting. Although she valiantly played the role of good reporter, the articles she wrote were mostly confined to the art world. She made the best of it and made them edgier, too. Her focus on artists' struggles ruffled feathers among the city's elite. "It is certainly time for people to wake up to the fact that there is beauty in other things than the face of a dollar," she wrote, chastising the rich for their ambivalence towards the arts. She urged the city to open a gallery exhibiting local work, which it did.

While influential, the assignments weren't what Bly had hoped for. Obviously frustrated, one day she just never showed up at her desk. By the time her coworkers found the note she left behind for them, Bly was already on a train to New York City. "Look out for me!" the note read.

In New York, there was no shortage of newspapers from which to choose, but Bly wanted to work for *The World*, mostly because of the man who was running it. His name was Joseph Pulitzer and

Nellie Bly. The Library of Congress [1890].

his reputation preceded him. Pulitzer had bought the struggling *World* newspaper from financier Jay Gould and made it an instant success. Mixing provocative headlines and gritty illustrations, *The World* soon surpassed mainstay stalwart dailies like *The New York Sun* and *The New York Herald* in both sales and revenue.

In a sly attempt to get noticed, Bly posed as a reporter and propositioned interviews with the city's top newspapermen. Bly explained she was writing an article about women in the workplace. Her objective came in the guise of a question: *Is New York a good place for a woman journalist to get a start?* Bly set up meetings and met with some of New York's best "voices." She wasn't being deceptive. Bly had kept ties with the *Dispatch* back in Pittsburgh and was writing and sending articles, mostly features on women. The story she wrote was effective. It included each response verbatim, with just a little commentary thrown in for good measure. "Take some girls that have the ability, procure for them situations, start them on their way, and by so doing accomplish more than by years of talking," Bly wrote. Not surprisingly, most of the men denied there was any prejudice against women. It got worse from there. Charles A. Dana of *The Sun* told Bly that women reporters were "not regarded with editorial favor in New York." He claimed a woman may not be as accurate as men in reporting, a key to success as a journalist. At this, Bly added, "I groaned mentally at the fate of this interview."

Bly's contact at *The World* was Colonel John A. Cockerill, Pulitzer's chief editor. Here she hoped to gain a lead on a possible job offer, but instead found only the same disappointing viewpoint. Cockerill told her that women in general "are not fit or do not want to cover the hard news," then added, "a man is of far greater service." However, he did point out that the paper employed two women on their staff. "See, we do not object personally," he added.

The article published in the *Dispatch* was reprinted in two of New York's smaller newspapers, *The Mail* and *Express,* and distributed in smaller cities throughout the nation. Unfortunately, it wasn't the bombshell Bly was hoping for because the prevailing male chauvinistic attitude towards women workers was not a new topic. Earlier that year, another writer named Ida M. Tarbell called out the male domination of the newspaper world with a blistering editorial in *The Chautauquan,* a magazine of which she would later become managing editor: "Any woman who can do as strong and finished work as a man will find a position." It wasn't that simple. Even male counterparts who spoke out were punished for suggesting women didn't get their just rewards. Joseph Howard, Jr., coincidentally of *The World,* found that out the hard way. "On the subject of women in journalism," he wrote in his popular column titled *Howard Letters,* "one would imagine there are no successful women in the metropolitan field, but the editors are mistaken." With that bold pronouncement, Howard was fired.

Bly's tactics seemed to work. Her article not only showed how woefully misguided men could be, it also showcased Bly's ability to flesh out a story. If anyone were to hire a woman reporter now, she thought, why not her? So she knocked on *The World's* door again.

This time Cockerill, who had stubbornly refused her request for a job before, was more accommodating. He let Bly back in his office and listened to her story ideas and suggestions. Cockerill gave Bly his word that he would look them over but offered no other commitment. He didn't want to lose her interest, however, so he handed Bly $25 and told her not to reach out to any other newspaper. Bly complied, and soon enough she got the call. Cockerill had an idea: Bly would go undercover inside the shadowy walls of New York's notorious Blackwell Island, an infirmary for mostly insane women, or "lunatics," as mental patients were known at the time. Stories of abuses inside the Island were rampant but rarely substantiated. Bly would feign insanity, get admitted, and pose as a resident. It was as ambitious as it was intriguing—and risky too. Cockerill warned her of the consequences, perhaps heightening the awareness. Her life could be threatened by other "inmates," or she might face the prospect of starvation. Her imagination could conjure up the other dangers. If she could pull it off, Cockerill told her, "It's more than anyone would believe."

Bly didn't hesitate. She accepted the assignment, and two months later was in Blackwell Island observing, absorbing, and ultimately reporting. When she returned, *The World* ran a two-part series titled "Behind Asylum Bars." It was a huge hit and Bly got credit for it. Although bylines were rare, especially for a newcomer, there was Bly's name appearing in signature at the bottom. By the time the second installment was published, Nellie Bly was a part of the headline: *INSIDE THE MADHOUSE: Nellie Bly's Experience in the Blackwell Island Asylum.* From that point on, there was never a Nellie Bly story without her name attached to it.

Just a few months after the Blackwell Island series ran in the paper, the story came out as a book. Bly was a story too, not just for her hard-hitting reporting, but for her meteoric rise to the top, something unheard of for a woman journalist. Bly was a new national star.

Soon she would become internationally famous as well.

3

I may pursue
other routes

〜♪ In the fall of 1888, while Bly was at home thinking of potential stories, the idea of traveling around the world faster than
Verne's fictional Phileas Fogg suddenly came to her. Being a fan
of Jules Verne and the book, she was intrigued by the thought of
recreating and breaking Fogg's record. *Had anyone even tried?* Bly
couldn't wait to go into work the next day and present her idea to
Cockerill. The stunt, or at least some variation of it, had already
been discussed, but no one considered a woman making the trip. A
man, Cockerill implied, could go alone, but a lady, at least a proper one, would need an escort. Plus, he added, a woman would be
weighted down with more baggage, something he meant literally. Bly was furious. "Start the man and I'll start the same day for
another newspaper and beat him," she countered.

Bly was dead serious and Cockerill knew it. She stated her case
and insisted she would travel light, but needed to do it alone. Cockerill told Bly that if they ever decided to go ahead with the plan, the
assignment would be hers—a promise he would keep despite receiving offers from a half-dozen men who said they would be willing
to make the mad dash around the globe. Bly left the office hopeful.

Although the globe-trotting trip was always in the back of her
mind, she continued to work and make headlines for her investi-

gative reporting. Then, acting on a suggestion, she lightened it up a bit. Bly began a series highlighting the often colorful, but seemingly unladylike, activities that New York City had to offer. She participated in a Wild West Show, played the cornet in a marching band, danced ballet, went ice skating, rode a bicycle, and spent the day at the Saratoga Racetrack, just to name a few. Bly's weekly stories featured headlines with her name first and the next adventure second.

Bly received hundreds of letters a week, some good and some bad and some even asking for her hand in marriage. With that kind of notoriety in place, in the fall of 1889, and nearly a full year after Bly had suggested it, Cockerill and the editorial board at *The World* made the decision that they would send their star reporter around the world. She was given word on November 11, a Monday, and told to pack immediately. If all went well, she would leave in three days.

Bly packed light as she had promised, taking a liberal amount of clothing, some toilet articles, her work tools like pen and copy paper, and the only thing she considered "bulky and compromising," a jar of cold cream. "The problem of baggage becomes a very simple one when one is traveling simply for the sake of traveling and not for the purpose of impressing one's fellow passengers," she wrote. Although it was discussed, she decided against carrying a revolver. Her most prized possession was a 24-hour dial pocket watch which would mark the time at which she left and again when she returned. At exactly 9:40:30 A.M. on Thursday, November 14, 1889, the White Star steamer *Augusta Victoria* pulled away from its moorings on Hoboken Pier in Jersey City, New Jersey, bound for England.

Nellie Bly was on board.

All this attention certainly didn't pass by the inquisitive Train, who must have followed Bly's exploits with a watchful eye. Whether Bly had any idea who Train was is not known. She mentions nothing of Train or his previous journey in her memoirs, and subsequent biographies of Bly treat Train's round-the-world trip with disdain rather than praise. Still, Train claimed it first and now it was Bly's turn. However, as much as Train may have thought of himself as a trailblazer in just about everything, not even he could claim the originality of traveling around the world.

That distinction goes to John Ledyard.

Ledyard, the son of a sea captain, was born in Groton, Connecticut, and attended Dartmouth College in New Hampshire before traveling to London and enlisting in the Royal Marines so he could assist England's great explorers. In 1778, while in his late 20s, Ledyard was appointed corporal on Captain James Cook's third and last voyage around the Pacific Rim. Unlike many of the other sailors on board, Ledyard was educated and literate, and kept a journal. When the ship *Resolution* returned to England without Cook, who had been killed—some say executed—by Hawaiian natives, Ledyard's firsthand account of the Captain's final days was confiscated by the Admiralty. Ledyard, however, had a story to tell and didn't hesitate to rewrite the details of Cook's murder from memory. The resulting book, *A Journal of Captain Cook's Last Voyage,* became a bestseller.

Despite all his successes, Ledyard still had the desire to see the world, possibly *all* of it if he could. In December of 1786, he set off alone from London, determined to be the first person to circle the globe. It was as crazy as it was ambitious, and Ledyard had another American to thank for it: a self-described "explorer aficionado" and a future president of the United States, Thomas Jefferson.

Jefferson proposed the idea of an American exploring America, specifically the uncharted land between the two lateral coasts. There had been no precedent for the journey, but at the time, reaching new milestones in exploration was tantamount to becoming a rock star today. Ledyard, however, considered the idea of simply exploring North America too easy. Perhaps circumnavigating the entire globe would be more functional, he opined. Jefferson, an ambassador in Paris at the time, had no objections. So with Jefferson's blessing, Ledyard mapped out a route. He would begin in London and trudge over land solely on foot, including walks across Russia and again through North America. He would sail over the Bering Strait and sail back again across the Atlantic to London.

For the first two months, everything went as planned. Ledyard

walked, begged for food and shelter along the way, and made it to
the Baltic Sea, the short inlet separating Scandinavia from northern Europe. Since the water had not frozen over as Ledyard had
hoped, walking across the ice was not an option. Instead, Ledyard
had to loop around the sea, mapping out nearly 400 miles more
just to reach St. Petersburg. The Arctic Circle was brutal, but Ledyard pressed on. By September of 1787, nearly 6,500 miles into his
journey and after enduring some of the harshest conditions imag-
inable, Ledyard made it to Russia, stepped onto Russian soil, and
was subsequently arrested.

This should not have come as a surprise to Ledyard. When planning the trip, Jefferson had asked the Russian leader Catherine the
Great for permission to cross her land unmolested. The Empress
flat out refused, worried that the American traveler–or any American–would infiltrate her country's lucrative fur trade. Jefferson
relayed this information to Ledyard, who chose to ignore it. Now
he was in Russia and in custody.

Russian officials marched him to the Polish border, set him free,
and promised to hang him if he ever set foot in their country again.
Ledyard was defiant. In his journal, he wrote, "I travel under the
common flag of humanity, commissioned by myself to serve the
world at large; and so the poor, the unprotected wanderer must go
where sovereign will ordains...why then the royal dame has taken
me much out of my way." But Ledyard still wanted to find a way.
"I may pursue other routes," he wrote. Perhaps the British royalty
would have more influence over Russia. So he turned his back on
Jefferson and went directly to London, where exclusive clubs and
societies were filled with men intent on one thing: funding explorations. His timing was impeccable. A new society called the African Association was looking for someone to lead a mission through
the African continent. Ledyard practically fell into their laps. He
accepted the assignment wholeheartedly.

Ledyard set off for Africa, but didn't make it very far. In 1789,
only three years after he began his journey around the world, Ledyard was dead. In Cairo, he had fallen ill, carelessly took a dangerous sulfurous acid to ease his stomach pain, and succumbed to an
overdose of the vitriolic substance.

Fifteen years later, in 1803, Jefferson funded another expedition, this time a team of two men who would chart the American West, his original plan for Ledyard. Their names were William Clark and Meriwether Lewis. Perhaps had Ledyard followed Jefferson's original plans, he would have been credited with exploring the expansion across the Continental Divide and the waterway to the Pacific that today is attributed to Lewis and Clark. Even in Africa, he might have been the first person to discover the source of the Nile, but he was too driven, too courageous, too stubborn. He wanted more and got far less. After his sudden death in 1789, neither the British nor the American authorities claimed Ledyard's body. In Cairo, his remains lie buried in a makeshift unmarked grave.

Ledyard's plan to literally circle the Earth would become more conceivable a century or so later when the railroads changed how we traveled across land. Suddenly the idea of making a trip around the world and in the shortest amount of time possible was a reality that an idealist like George Francis Train and a journalist like Nellie Bly couldn't wait to try. "The circumference of the globe had shrunken," Train later wrote in his biography. "I wanted naturally, to be the first man to utilize the great advantage this given to travel by making the quickest trip around the world." So he did, setting off on August 1, 1870, and sailing west from San Francisco to Yokohama, Japan, then aboard a U.S. ship *Alaska* from Saigon to Marseilles, where he was briefly jailed. "The remainder of the voyage was uneventful," he wrote. "I passed on rapidly to New York, and finished my tour inside of eighty days." Train's journey, he professed, was even more special because Verne copied it. However, his claim was deceptive. True, Train had spent only 80 days traveling, but not consecutively. He needed considerably more days to actually complete the task.

Nellie Bly, however, did it with time to spare.

On January 25, 1890, a Saturday, at exactly 3:51:44 P.M., Bly completed her globe-trotting journey in an astounding 73 days, quicker than the fictitious Fogg and most certainly faster than George Francis Train. She had traveled through London, France, Ceylon, Singapore, and Hong Kong, and arrived back to the U.S. aboard

Nellie Bly around the world. The Library of Congress [February 21, 1890].

the steamer *Oceanic*. In San Francisco, she was forced to take a special Santa Fe train due to heavy snowfalls in the Sierras which delayed the transcontinental line by nearly two days. By avoiding the main line, she made it to Chicago in 69 hours. The rest of the trip aboard the Pennsylvania Railroad line was academic. "Father Time Undone," *The World*'s headlines blared on Sunday, January 26, just a day after Bly had stepped off the train in Jersey City and ended her trip in a record breaking "72 days, 6 hours, 11 minutes, and 14 seconds." In that time, Bly had sent back weekly dispatches appearing in the Sunday paper that captivated readers from start to finish. Now that she had safely returned, the story had a remarkable footnote too. "Bly will never be misunderstood," the mayor of Jersey City, Orestes Cleveland, shouted to the masses upon her arrival. "She will be recognized as pushing, determined, independent, and able to take care of herself wherever she may go."

The Sunday editions of *The World* spread like wildfire, setting a print run record for one day of 280,340 copies. Bly was an international sensation, and soon the newspaper was receiving letters postmarked from Europe from mothers naming their newborns after her. The rail line she used on the last leg of the trip, the Pennsylvania Railroad, would later change the name of their fastest train between New York and Atlantic City to the *Nellie Bly Express*.

Even Train seemed to get caught up in the excitement. Inspired, he would reattempt his around-the-world jaunt all over again in 1890, shortly after Bly's. Train had told his friends he would make it in 62 days. He made it in 67. "This was then the fastest trip around the world," he bragged. Not satisfied, Train did it again in 1892, at the age of 63. This time, he completed the trip in 60 days. His acknowledgment of Bly's effort would come later in his book. "There had been some noteworthy efforts on the part of newspaper writers to make the record-breaking trip," Train wrote. He mentions Bly by name and another woman: Elizabeth Bisland.

Bly, as it turned out, had competition.

The same day Bly was set to leave, the editor of *Cosmopolitan* magazine, John Brisben Walker, had an idea. What if he sent off a reporter in the opposite direction of Bly, west through the continental U.S. and across the Pacific first? Walker thought that route might be quicker, but he had to hurry. Bly was departing and the only way to beat her was to leave on the same day. Walker knew there was no other choice than to send a woman. In a cramped apartment not far from the magazine's lower Manhattan headquarters, Elizabeth Bisland, a 28-year-old freelance writer for *Cosmopolitan,* best known for her weekly literary column "In the Library," was preparing for her day. She received an urgent message to meet Walker in his office. That very afternoon, Bisland boarded a train heading west.

Seventy-eight days later, on January 30, she was back in New York's Manhattan harbor. Seasick and wobbly from the long ocean voyage across the Atlantic, Bisland stepped onto the dock at the foot of Clarkson Street and fell into the arms of her sister Molly, who had been waiting at the end of the gangway. Bisland lost the race by four-and-a-half days, not a huge defeat, but a significant one, since the *Cosmopolitan* had billed it as a contest between the two women.

In retrospect, Walker had only himself to blame for sending Bisland in the opposite direction and thinking the headwinds in the South China Sea would work in her favor. As it turned out, he hadn't allowed for a more predicable weather pattern for Bisland's longest and final leg of the trip, a January crossing of the Atlantic that proved to be choppy and slow. Regardless of Walker's miscalculation, considering the day she left Liverpool, Bisland likely wouldn't have made it even in better weather. Most ships could complete a voyage from Europe to America in 11 days. To beat Bly, she would have had to break the existing sailing record of seven days, a record that was set in May, not January. While Bisland's homebound ship was battling the waves and dodging ice fields to make it home, Bly, who had sailed the Atlantic in November, was riding comfortably on a train instead.

Though Bly enjoyed the rewards of her unprecedented fame, the most fulfilling part of the trip came in France when she got to meet Jules Verne. Thanks to *The World,* Verne agreed to host her at his home just outside of Paris. Bly excitedly accepted. "A bright fire was crackling," she later wrote, "throwing a soft, warm light over the room." Verne spoke little English, so they conversed through a translator. Bly asked Verne how he came up with the idea for Fogg's adventure. "I got it from a newspaper," Verne replied, describing an article of calculations that showed the journey could be completed in 80 days. "The idea pleased me and while thinking it over struck me that in their calculations they had not called into account the difference in the meridians. So I went to work to write one." Bly was given a tour of Verne's study and was struck by a manuscript with several sentences crossed out. "Verne always improved his work by taking out superfluous things," she wrote. In the end, Verne gave his blessing and wished her well. "If you do it in 79 days," he told her, "I shall applaud you with both hands."

Later, Verne would fondly recall the visit. "Nobody, to look at the quiet, ladylike little thing, would have thought for a moment that she was what she is and that she was going to do what she was doing," he wrote. Verne's book had been out for two decades, but after Bly's journey was over, new editions of *Around the World in Eighty Days* were reprinted in several languages and an updated stage production was in the works.

Verne's interest in long-distance travel extended beyond Fogg's many adventures. In 1863, he released a book titled *Five Weeks in a Balloon* about an imaginary hydrogen-filled balloon expedition across the continent of Africa, then under British rule. The book was full of enough scientific and statistical data to convince readers it could actually be done. Verne was on to something, as was John Wise before him. Wise may have been the first person to fly a balloon over Niagara Falls, but he never made it across the Atlantic Ocean by air, as he had hoped. He also never achieved the more realistic dream of flying over the full continental United States, a fictional feat Verne describes in his 1875 novel, *The Mysterious Island*. That story begins in 1865 as a group of Union soldiers commandeer a balloon and escape the Southern capitol, Richmond, where they were being detained. A strong easterly wind carries the men across America's plains, deserts, and mountains, and eventually over the Pacific where they land on an uncharted island "seven thousand miles from their home." Verne's story was published nearly a quarter of century before Nellie Bly went around the world, but even then, neither Bly herself nor her editor's at *The World* considered a balloon a viable source of travel. That would not change. In fact, no one would achieve a nonstop transcontinental trip by balloon in the 19th century and, for that matter, most of the 20th century too. By the first quarter of the new century, however, it didn't matter. Even Bly's record would become insignificant, due to an advance in travel that had nothing to do with water or land. Thanks to a man named Amos Root, and his curious–almost obsessive–interest in contraptions, the unsuspecting public was about to find out why.

And it all starts with bees.

4
I have a wonderful story to tell you

⌐⌐⌐ Amos Ives Root was known as "The Bee Man," not only because he harvested bees, but because he collected and studied them as well. Root grew up on a farm in Medina, Ohio, a rural community just west of Akron, where he helped his mother plant flowers and vegetables in the family's garden. Perhaps due to Root being small in size and prone to sickness, the gardening work held a deep connection for the young boy. He developed an intense love for everything involving nature and a curiosity for science. "I have been all my life much given to hobbies and projects," he would later write.

Studies came easy, and in his late teens, Root became passionate about electricity and magnetism, a technology just beginning to emerge. He left home and toured the Midwest, giving demonstrations and lessons, but it was a steady income that Root needed. He took up jewelry as a trade and became quite good at it. He married, eventually raising five children, and opened a jewelry shop in town to support a family. That's when he discovered bees. Actually, they discovered him, lots of them, swarming above the shop's door like uninvited guests. Intrigued rather than annoyed, Root watched their "habits" from a distance. A worker at the shop noticed Root's interest and asked if he wanted to see them up close.

The bees? Root thought, surprised. "How much would you give for them?" the worker inquired. Root offered him a dollar. "To my astonishment," Root would later recall, "he [the worker], in a short time, returned with them in a rough box he had heartily picked up." Root was entranced: "Before night I had questioned not only the bees, but everyone I knew who could tell me something about these new acquaintances of mine."

Eventually, his work led to founding a national trade journal titled *Gleanings in Bee Culture*. Root was the editor and wrote most of the articles. Root was also a devout Christian, a temperance activist, and one of the founding benefactors of the Anti-Saloon League. Bees, though, were his main focus. Many in town thought his bee infatuation was fleeting, but when Root started the journal and began paying employees to look after the bees, they quickly changed their minds. The bee work turned profitable. Root found a way to extract honey and still save the bees during the winter. This led to a wax candle factory in town, the A.I. Root Company.

Root always had his hand in something innovative. He was one of the first in Medina to ride a high-wheeler bicycle, oftentimes failing in the process. He may have been ridiculed for his efforts, a friend explained, but "went straight to his work without faltering or swerving from the path he had chosen." This attitude is what may have drawn him to two minister's sons who owned a bicycle shop in Dayton. Root had read sketchy reports of the brothers' experiments in the newspapers. Although he had misguided information about what they were doing, he was intrigued nonetheless.

By this time, Root had picked up another obsession: the automobile. The contraption was a blessing for someone who hated cleaning up after a horse. "I do not like the smell of the stables," Root once wrote. But the automobile was different. "It never gets tired; it gets there quicker than any horse can possibly do." He bought an Oldsmobile Runabout "for less than a horse," he bragged. Root preached that the automobile was "a wonderful gift to the children of this age from the great Father above." Others weren't so sure. They found the machines loud, smelly, and unruly. Besides, they were symbols of the rich, something Root, who was very wealthy, could not argue. However, Root didn't mind being a lone wolf on the matter. He drove his Runabout constantly about town and wrote about its many pleasures in the bee journal.

Root's work with bees eventually ended. Now in his 60s, he bequeathed the day-to-day operations of the factory to his sons. Root kept busy tinkering with his toys instead, especially his beloved Runabout. In September 1904, at the age of 69, Root took his longest trip yet, a nearly 400-mile journey to Dayton to visit the two minister's sons. On impulse and curiosity, Root wrote them and asked if he could take a look. The brothers agreed, but only if he promised not to reveal any secrets. Root willingly obliged. His first words in the journal revealed little about why he was going or who he was going to meet. The purpose of the trip, he wrote, was "with the view of studying humanity," meaning man's attitude toward cars and horses, and the "question of automobiles on public roads." The first visit he watched in awe, but revealed nothing. The second trip he was given permission to write about what he had seen. It was the first time Orville and Wilbur Wright and their flying machine had been observed and the first eyewitness account to be published. "My dear friends," Root gleefully wrote in his bee publication, "I have a wonderful story to tell you."

Since Root's article appeared in print on January 1, 1905, the publication seems ridiculously anticlimactic. Thirteen months had passed since the Wright Brothers' triumphant flight at Kitty Hawk, North Carolina, the famous "fifty-seven seconds" for which they are most remembered today. As historically significant as it proved to be, that moment was witnessed by only a few bystanders. By their own design, the Wrights did their work covertly and the location of the first experiments was miles from nowhere. But on December 17, 1903, they successfully completed the first manned flight and couldn't wait to share the news with family and friends. On that same day, a telegram arrived at the Wright family home back in Ohio. Another Wright brother, Lorin, hand-delivered the report to the *Dayton Journal* with an incredible proclamation: Man could fly! It was rejected. "Fifty-seven seconds," the city editor told Lorin upon reading the report, "if it had been fifty-seven minutes we might have a story." The name of the editor, who also represented the Associated Press, is not lost to time, but not much else is known about Frank Tunison, the man who flatly noted that the Wright Brothers' first flight was inadmissible.

The Wrights felt the sting of rejection from their hometown paper, and the reports that did appear from across the nation were just flat-out wrong. The Wrights wanted to be recognized for their efforts, not dismissed as attention-seeking hacks. When they sent the telegram from Kitty Hawk to the weather station in Norfolk with orders to send it directly to Dayton, they specifically told the operator on duty that the information was extremely "confidential." When the operator read the telegram, he ignored the order at first and wired the brothers back, asking for permission to share the news with a friend at the *Virginian-Pilot*. It's conceivable that the operator Joseph Dosher didn't wait for a response from the Wrights and excitedly let his newspaper friend in on the secret. "Flying Machine Soars over 3 Miles in Teeth of High Winds Over Sand Hills and Waves over Kitty Hawk" was the headline in the *Virginian-Pilot* the next day. The brothers were furious. Not only was the headline factually wrong (in actuality, the flight was just a little over 800 feet), but the rest of the story was filled with misinformation and contrived scenarios as well. "Eureka!" the paper reported Wilber shouting at one point, even though he most certainly did not.

The story in the *Virginian-Pilot* was picked up by other newspapers in major cities like New York, Chicago, and Cincinnati, but hardly anyone noticed. No one knew who the Wright Brothers were and a kite powered by a motor was just plain absurd. "The machine has no balloon attachment," the AP reported.

This is when Amos Root got wind of the experiments in Dayton. Thanks to his persistence and a healthy readership for the bee publication, the world finally read the truth about the two brothers and their amazing flying machine. "It was my privilege, on the 20th day of September, 1904 to see the first successful trip of an airship," he wrote with conviction.

Perhaps there would have been no interest at all in the story had it not been for the failures of others, particularly Samuel Pierpont

Langley, one of the most prominent scientists in the nation in the late 19th century. Langley envisioned lighter-than-air flight by building an "aerodrome," a name he coined from the Greeks, which meant "air runner." Technically, sustained flight had been conquered by balloons, but Langley envisioned more. He wanted flight that was powered and controlled too. The aerodrome then was essentially a cross-sectioned frame with a large hull to support the engine and arms—or wings—to each side, which held propellers. Langley knew that balance and steering would be the main issue. Add the weight of a steam engine and it was anyone's guess if the craft would even lift off the ground.

Langley had the influential 17th-century mathematician and astronomer Isaac Newton to blame for planting the seed of doubt. Newton contended that artificial flight could not be obtained because the power needed to sustain it lay beyond the reach of man. Langley scoffed at such notions, but still he was cautious. Initial tests on hand models were disappointing, but he could wait no longer. Hours in the lab produced a specimen at least, but it was unproven. Langley figured the only way to find out was to give it a try, so he did over the still waters of the Potomac River in a suitably wide section near the town of Quantico, Virginia. Langley built a launcher to catapult the aerodrome in the air before the engines would do the rest. To assure the craft started over the water, the launcher was placed upon the deck of a houseboat. The location was fitting since several months before, Langley had spent hours on another houseboat in Crepe Benton, Nova Scotia, where a good friend, Alexander Graham Bell, lived on a lavish grand estate overlooking the scenic cape. Bell, who had been conducting flight experiments of his own, would be on hand in Virginia to help.

On May 6, 1896, two Langley aerodromes were let loose. The first one never made it off the launcher. A guide wire broke, snapping a wing in the process and sending the craft crashing into the water, crushing the propellers upon impact. The next one shot out of the catapult and rose to about 20 feet in height. It seemed to dip at first, which elicited a disheartening sigh from the spectators that lined the banks. Then, as the propellers gave it thrust, the craft pushed slowly forward, making a spiral nearly 100 feet

Samuel Pierpont Langley. The Library of Congress, part of the Harris and Ewing Collection [1913].

in diameter before the steam ran out. Bell looked on in disbelief. He expected the craft to nosedive into the water with a splash, but instead, like a gull, the aerodrome performed a feat of flight, higher and longer than any previous attempts. The result was encouraging, but not satisfying enough. Yes, Langley had successfully put a power source on a craft and propelled it some distance, but it was no "soaring bird" as he and others had claimed they could build.

This "soaring bird" assertion dated back to 1886, when Langley first became interested in flight. That's the year he attended the convention of the American Association of the Advancement of Science in Buffalo, New York, an organization made up of high-minded truth-seekers. Mostly university professors and the like, members of the association were intent on furthering the elite standards of scholarly thinking, while at the same time debunking theories from those who undercut their efforts. Langley fit right in.

The convention was well attended—3,000 or more were present —and meticulously planned and detailed. Every aspect of the scientific community would be represented, including mathematics, astronomy, physics, chemistry, mechanical science and engineering, geology, geography, zoology, botany, anthropology, and social and economic science. When the Mechanical Science and Engineering portion of the program started, Octave Chanute, the highly regarded French-American civil engineer, spoke in length about advancements in engines and motors before turning specifically to the matter of powered flying machines. "The difficulties in the way of success are very great," he explained. "Yet there are so many sober men who expect eventual success.

"You will at this meeting listen to a paper by a proper gentleman who has devoted five years of his life solely to the flight of birds," Chanute continued. "He is convinced that it [mechanical flight] is accomplished with an expenditure of muscular power far less than previously supposed." Israel Lancaster now had his turn. Listed by the *Times* as "Prof. Lancaster," Lancaster may have been a Midwestern farmer, although no one was quite sure. Chanute had invited him to the convention, perhaps to make a point. Lancaster explained that he could build a mechanical bird that could soar like the real thing—or for 15 minutes, at least. "The capacity of the room was almost too small for the demands upon it," the *Times* reported. Lancaster brought out a model of this "soaring bird" machine and was nearly laughed off the stage. It was a simple wooden frame with an iron bar and scales, certainly nothing that impressed a roomful of scientists. Lancaster tried to convince the crowd by waving sheets of diagrams and explaining his theories, but to no avail. The mathematicians and mechanical engineers were having none of it. They asked him a few technical questions but, according to the *Times,* received "unsatisfactory answers."

Enough was enough. The President of the AAAS, Professor Edward S. Morse, a successful zoologist whose main study was seashells, rose to claim the audience back. Morse asked Lancaster that if he could build one as quickly as he proposed, why hadn't he shown one. A man stood from the audience and offered a $100 bill if Lancaster would "make a model of a soaring bird that would work." Another man upped the offer to $1,000. "The model of the soaring birds would so far have to overcome the law of gravitation as to fall up instead of down," one man chided.

In the audience listening was Langley, who at the age of 57 was considered one of the leading experts in astronomy. He ran the day-to-day operations of the prestigious Alleghany Observatory in Pittsburgh, where he studied—but had not settled on—the stars and planets as his only means of contentment. To a scientific mind, Pittsburgh was a frustrating town. Resources like books, periodicals, and manuals were scarce in a city built on its industrial base. "There are not only no museums of art, no libraries of reference, no collections of scientific material," Langley said frustratingly, "but in general, none of the aids to the investigator which are to be found in many younger and smaller places."

This was the same Pittsburgh where Nellie Bly was writing stories for the local *Dispatch.* Langley's motivation was different from Bly's. He often escaped the city and the observatory just to free his mind. That's why, in 1886, he was on hand in Buffalo to witness poor Lancaster get berated by his peers. Instead of anger, however, Langley was inspired. "Soaring birds" made him think of hawks he used to watch as a child, soaring majestically over his head.

While the idea of flight consumed him, Langley was in no hurry.

That fall, only months after the convention, Langley left his post at the observatory to become head of the international exchange division of the Smithsonian Institute in Washington, D.C. Change was good for Langley, and leaving the isolation of Pittsburgh was even better. In Washington, he could do research and continue his quest to build a machine that could fly. The following year, Spencer Baird, the longtime secretary of the Smithsonian, died, and Langley took over. Langley was busy and preoccupied, and it wouldn't be until May of 1896, some 10 years past the Buffalo convention, that Langley tested his first aerodrome to disappointing results.

Around this same time, the Wright Brothers were secretly testing kites in their Dayton bicycle shop. Octave Chanute, the man Langley listened to lament the prospects of engine-powered flight at the convention, and the Wrights were corresponding. In 1890, Wilbur wrote Chanute, asking for advice as to where they should test their new winged flyer and whether or not any others had attempted or failed in doing the same. Wilbur was clear that his intention was not to get rich by being the first to do so, but that "those who were willing to give as well as to receive suggestions can hope to link their names with the honor of its discovery." Chanute likely did not need to fill the Wrights in on Langley's efforts, which were widely known, but apparently left Langley in the dark as to what the Wrights were doing.

On October 7, 1903, Langley was ready to test his new and improved aerodrome again from the same houseboat and spot on the Potomac River. This time, Langley had a partner, a mechanic named Charles Manly, who helped the scientist build a more efficient, lighter, and more powerful engine. Unlike in the first attempts, Manly would also be on board the craft, manning the controls. A large crowd was on hand to witness the event, and both Langley and Manly were confident this modified flyer would indeed soar like a bird. Manly, who sat in the center of the craft, waited for the signal. When the stay wires were removed and the counterweight flung back, the machine took off over the river, clearing the track and dropping like a rock straight down into the water. Manly barely escaped.

The next day, the *New York Times* wrote an editorial which blamed Langley for wasting everyone's time. "This ridiculous fiasco which attended the attempt at aerial navigation in the Langley flying machine was not unexpected," the editor wrote, "unless possibly by the distinguished Secretary of the Smithsonian who devised it, and his assistant." Langley defended his flying machine and blamed a flaw in the launching mechanism which, he explained, drew the machine downward instead of up. This was certainly something Langley could correct and two months later, on December 6, he set out to prove it.

Manly was once again at the controls and once again the flyer bolted off the catapult's track, hung only briefly over the river, turned completely over, and flopped into the water on its back. This time, Manly was trapped and needed to be rescued by one of Langley's helpers. Langley still insisted the launcher was the problem, not the aerodrome. Others weren't so sure. Later, when the physics of flight were better understood, it was determined that Langley, who had no formal mathematics or engineering education, needed more power to generate more lift, either in the engine or the launcher. Nevertheless, Langley was defeated again. He insisted he would give it another try, but the government grant money he received, nearly $50,000, had run out and no one was willing to spend any more federal funds on a failing enterprise.

Keeping tabs from afar in Kitty Hawk were the Wright Brothers. They didn't know Langley personally, but had heard about the latest failure. Wilbur immediately sent a letter to Chanute. "It seems to be our turn now," he wrote, "and I wonder what our luck would be." On December 17, only 11 days after Langley's second debacle, the Wright Brothers flew 57 seconds into history with no one there to witness it. Well, no one, that is, except a few Coast Guardsmen who helped carry the plane's parts up the hill and a man named John Daniels, a local resident, who became the Wrights' impromptu photographer.

Just over a year later, Amos Root would change all that. "They have twice succeeded in making four complete circles without alighting, each circle passing the starting-point," he wrote. "These circles are nearly a mile in circumference each more to convince others they were not just flying, but in charge of it as well." His obvious regard for their work was infectious: "When Columbus discovered America he did not know what the outcome would be, and no one at the time knew; and I doubt if the wildest enthusiast caught a glimpse of what really did come from his discovery. In a like manner, these brothers have probably not even a faint glimpse of what their discovery is going to bring to the children of men."

In 1908, the Wright Brothers went to France and became internationally famous. There, in front of enthusiastic crowds, they demonstrated their improved flying machine by performing circles, banking turns, and landing at the same spot they started. Since then, their first flight at Kitty Hawk has been defined as *the* landmark moment in the history of aviation.

Langley, on the other hand, had no such luck. After his second failed attempt to get his aerodrome to fly, he never got another chance. His health deteriorated and two years later, he was dead. In regard to aviation, his name became synonymous with failure. Only his friend Alexander Graham Bell gave Langley credit for "demonstrating to the world the practicality of mechanical flight." Bell's carefully chosen words here were entirely correct. Langley had shown that he had created the first flying machine capable of carrying an engine and eventually a man; problem was, it just didn't fly. "There was nothing the matter with it," Bell explained. "It stuck in the launching ways, and the public were no more justified in supposing that it could not fly, than they would be were they to suppose that because a ship stuck in the launching ways it could not float." Again, the choice of words, and particularly the analogy, was solid, but not everyone bought Bell's high-minded praise. A scathing editorial in the *Chicago Tribune* chastised Bell and compared the aerodrome to a duck who can also point its nose down and dive: "The principal difference is the duck can come up without ruffling a feather, while the aerodrome stays down in the mud and is dragged up piece by piece."

Bell was personally offended. Had the two brothers from Dayton been publicly scrutinized from the beginning, he argued, perhaps their early failures would also have been subject to the same criticism that Langley experienced. After Langley's death, Bell set out to make a flying machine of his own, but as history knows, his life's work, which included one of the most significant discoveries of the 19th century, puts him in another field of invention.

As planes modeled after the initial Wright flyer were improved and perfected, the quest to fly only became more intense. Just as it had been a century before when the railroad made the world a smaller place, the idea of breaking barriers was the issue. The aircraft had its limitations, however. It still needed an open patch of solid ground to start and stop. Flying great distances, like across the world's oceans, remained obstacles yet to be conquered. Thus, mankind's reliance on ships to move goods and people between continents would continue for decades. And like the later race to fly, the need for speed and superiority on the Atlantic was just as vexing and ultimately rewarding. This is due in part to a British man named Isambard Kingdom Brunel.

5

Why not make
it longer?

⌯⌯ On June 13, 1842, Queen Victoria took her first train ride
aboard a locomotive named *Phlegethon* along the newly christened
Great Western Railway, England's longest and most ambitious rail
line to date. The trip from London to Slough near Windsor Castle
took less than half an hour. Impressed, the Queen wrote in her
diary, "The motion was very slight and much easier than the carriage, also no dust or great heat...it was so quick." When asked for
a comment, the Queen gave a more proper, but still enthusiastic
response. "I am quite charmed by it," she said.

Built nearly 20 years before the U.S.'s first transcontinental
railroad, but not nearly its equivalent in length, England's Great
Western Railway was significant because of its concept and design,
not its size. From elaborate bridges to seemingly inconceivable tunnels, the Great Western was an engineering marvel. One man gets
credit for that: Isambard Kingdom Brunel.

Born in Portsmouth, England, to French and English parents,
Brunel grew to be only five feet tall as an adult, a genetic trait he
inherited from his father, Marc Brunel, who may have been short
in height, but was long on ideas. A machinist and civic and mechanical engineer, the elder Brunel built bridges throughout England
and mined tunnels under the Thames River. A teenage Isambard
helped. "So gifted was young Brunel and such was the intelligence

and enthusiasm which he brought to bear upon his father's projects that in spite of his youth he rapidly became more of a trusted and able partner than an assistant," wrote Brunel biographer L.T.C. Rolt.

Brunel's meticulous approach to detail, especially his knack for figuring out seemingly insurmountable problems, would eventually become his trademark. During the construction of the Great Western, Brunel was confronted by a steep bank hill near Bath, which graded the landscape to the point no track could be laid. Brunel chose to go through it instead, carving out a nearly two-mile tunnel into mostly solid bedrock. The tunnel alone took five years to complete, involved 4,000 workmen, and cost nearly 100 lives. The Box Tunnel, named for the hill through which it went, was the longest railway tunnel in the world.

Brunel loved the spotlight and often bragged about how he and only he knew how to make and fix things. Even while the rail line was being built, Brunel put his engineering skills to work in other ventures, specifically steamships. During a meeting for the planning of the Great Western in 1835, an objection was made as to its length. Why spend all the time and labor boring all the holes for tunnels near the end of the proposed line when you can end the line before the obstacles begin and be done with it? Brunel rebuked them. "Why not make it longer, and have a steamboat to go from Bristol to New York?" he responded half-jokingly. After the laughter died down, a few entrepreneurial types took Brunel up on his offer and the Great Western Steam Ship Company was born.

Like a good engineer, Brunel tried to figure out how to move a steamship faster and more efficiently. First, attitudes had to change. Until then, the idea of a ship that sailed across the open sea by an engine alone was simply not workable, either due to space or weight restriction. Brunel showed it could be done by simply lengthening the ship. Invoking a common shipbuilding principle that a vessel's resistance did not increase with its size, Brunel insisted that a ship with extra tonnage (interior space) and room to carry a large amount of coal and machinery would do the job. In theory, with more capacity to store coal, say 580 tons, on a steamship that weighed 1,200 tons and an engine that generated

300 horsepower, a ship could maintain a constant speed of six to nine knots and cross the Atlantic in just 13 days—less than half the current voyage time by sail. The Great Western Steam Ship Company planned to build two boats that size, but changed the plan. They would go grander in scale and build one large ship that weighed 1,400 tons and generated 400 horsepower.

Brunel, however, wasn't the only one computing the physics of ocean travel. Several competing shipbuilders both in England and abroad were also planning on putting ships on the water capable of using just steam engines to propel them. While others bickered over size and cost, leading to bankruptcies and broken promises, the Great Western Company's plan to build one ship continued unabated and served to put them far ahead in the race to steam across the Atlantic. In the spring of 1838, after only two years of planning and construction, the *Great Western,* the largest steamship of its kind in the world, was ready for her maiden voyage.

At eight minutes past six on the morning of the last day of March 1838, the *Great Western* left moorings on the Thames and headed for open waters. She was bound for New York by way of Bristol, where 50 passengers would be waiting to board. Not to be outdone, a rival ship company sent a smaller ship named *Sirius* out to compete with her. *Sirius* was less than half the size of Brunel's ship, and considered only a charter for its runs between London and Dublin. Modified for a transatlantic trip, it left three days before the *Great Western.* The *Sirius* had one problem that Brunel's ship did not: it could not make the voyage across the ocean without a final stop for coal, costing at least a day's time. Due to this delay, Brunel was convinced that the *Great Western* would pass the smaller ship in due course.

But not everything went as planned. Two hours into its maiden voyage, and while the ship was still in the Thames, fire broke out in the ship's boiler room. The *Great Western* was docked again, this time wasting a precious 12 hours before the blaze was snuffed out. By the time she reached the boarding dock in Bristol, word of the fire had spread and nearly all of the 50 people who had purchased tickets cancelled. Despite this, on April 8, and after another frustrating day delayed due to weather, Brunel, the 57 crewmembers,

Isambard Kingdom Brunel. The Metropolitan Museum of Art, Robert Howlett, photographer, public domain.

and a handful of paid riders ("seven brave pioneers") steamed into the Atlantic bound for the American shore. "The hopes and goodwill of the city went with her," Rolt wrote, "but commercially her departure could not have been less auspicious."

The fire had detained the *Great Western* just long enough to enable the *Sirius* to narrowly win the race to New York. However, by the time the *Sirius* pulled into Long Island Harbor on April 22, after 19 days at sea, the coal had run so short that rumors persisted that the crew used wood paneling and other furniture parts to keep the fire stoked. On top of that, those onboard the *Sirius* were less than willing participants. After encountering brutal headwinds that sent the bow of the ship skyward before crashing back down in the heavy swells, the passengers implored the captain to abandon the trip and turn back. The captain's steadfast stubbornness was rewarded: New Yorkers greeted the *Sirius* with enthusiastic cheers and proved at least initially that the practicality of steam-powered ocean navigation was possible.

Literally within hours of the *Sirius'* arrival, the *Great Western* pulled into port. At first, it was unheralded, but as the numbers added up, Brunel's grand ship was vindicated. Not only had the *Great Western* made the ocean portion of the voyage in less time than the *Sirius,* just 15 days and 5 hours, the fastest crossing ever, it had also tackled the same headwinds without incident and with little complaint from the passengers and crew. Plus, she arrived with 200 tons of coal left in her bunkers, compared to only 15 tons left on the *Sirius.* Brunel's *Great Western* was gaining on the smaller ship at a rate of over two knots per hour. Had there been more sea to navigate and another day to make up, she might have surpassed the fuel-strapped *Sirius* with ease. "The achievement of the *Sirius* might have been dismissed as a bold stunt," wrote Rolt, "but the appearance of the *Great Western* on the afternoon of the same day convinced America that this was no freak exploit but the inauguration of a new era of rapid and reliable transport between the old world and the new." The *Great Western* would make the sea voyage back and forth five more times in 1838, each time carrying more passengers and completing nearly each trip faster than the previous. Continuous steam travel across the ocean had arrived and, despite such dangers as exploding boilers, more people accepted the risk in exchange for speed and consistency.

Brunel would help the Great Western Steam Company build more ships, but none would match the excitement and vitality associated with the first. In fact, the other ships like the *Great Britain* and the *Great Eastern* were considered "distinguished failures," especially the latter, which was built considerably larger than the *Great Western* but sorely underpowered, costly, and accident-prone, too. These projects, the author of *The Ocean Railway* Stephen Fox conceded, were "riddled with endless delays, revisions and spiraling costs."

The disappointments of the ships that followed the *Great Western* were not entirely Brunel's fault. As usual, he sought to build the perfect ship, but eventually time and money were factors he could not control. Other ship lines used the *Great Western*'s success as a springboard to monopolize the market. The names of these other shipbuilders, like Bruce Ismay of the White Star Line, have more familiarity due in part to their connection with tragedies, but it was Brunel—a revered figure in English history today but a virtual unknown in the U.S.—who had the vision to imagine moving people faster over oceans and between continents.

When it came to speed, durability, and longevity, however, one name stands out: Cunard.

Known as "Sam" to his friends and associates, Samuel Cunard was Canadian, born of German and Irish descent. He inherited the business of ship-making from his father, Abraham, the founder of the A. Cunard & Son company. Although the elder Cunard had three sons, Sam, who had experience working the merchants' docks, was the one referenced in the title. When Abraham died in 1824, Sam changed the name to the Samuel Cunard & Co. and enlisted his two brothers, Edward and Joseph, to join him. Though the family business, now exclusively run by Sam, included ship-making, iron and coal mining, landowning, property management, banking, and even whaling, the shipping part of the enterprise would be the most successful. Cunard soon amassed a large fleet of wooden ships for transporting and trading goods up and down the

Eastern coastline. Nearly all the ships he named after his mother and wife. The *Margarets* and *Susans* soon earned Cunard a fortune. But bigger was better, as Brunel had proved, and Cunard wanted to get his hands on the transatlantic money. He went to England to take a look.

The British government was busy making plans of its own. Impressed by the success of the *Great Western* but still leery of sending large numbers of people abroad on steam-powered vessels, they hoped to utililize the ships to carry the mail also. After learning the Admiralty had asked smaller English contractors, commissioned by the Royal Navy, to design and build steamships that on paper at least seemed far inferior, the Great Western Steam Company offered its services. The British government could do themselves a favor by choosing an established steamship company, but they would have to wait at least two years, the Great Western Steam Company explained. That way, they could build three boats, slightly smaller in size, but with more horsepower. Eager to proceed, the Admiralty rejected the offer and carried on with original plans to commission the building of its own ships and set the oceanic mail route in motion within months rather than years. Cunard arrived on British soil and made an offer. He could run enough of his ships to maintain a weekly service and put the previous mail ships, including the slower American packet boats, out of business. The plan was as devious as it was ambitious. Eventually, the British agreed to a twice monthly run and Cunard, who looked to make the most out of the deal, was in the transatlantic steam navigation business.

Cunard's regular mail and passenger service fleet was introduced with the *Britannia*, a smaller ship than the *Great Western*, but sleeker and faster thanks to a new engine design which reduced coal consumption and doubled power. The *Britannia*'s maiden voyage was in July of 1840. It averaged an eastbound trip in just 10 days, effectively putting Brunel and the Great Western Steam Company to shame. The *Britannia* is also the ship that carried Charles Dickens to the United States in January of 1842, a trip which resulted in his travel book, *American Notes,* and as previously mentioned a glowing and spiritual experience at Niagara Falls.

Dickens' description of transatlantic steamship travel, however, wasn't quite as complimentary. The accommodations were too small ("An utterly impracticable, thoroughly hopeless, and profoundly preposterous box"), too dismal-looking ("Not unlike a giant hearse with windows in the sides"), and too cold ("Three or four chilly stewards were warming their hands [over a 'melancholy' stove]"). The weather was exceptionally rough. A winter's gale blew that swayed the boat so violently it sent everyone, including Dickens and his wife, back to their staterooms. While Dickens' book was a potential cautionary tale for those wishing to travel by steamship across the ocean, it nevertheless did not slow down business. Many understood that weather could be a significant factor in a sea voyage. Dickens had never sailed by sea. His journey, while a personal hell, was not indicative of ocean travel as a whole. Others would find calmer seas, usually in the springtime, and since the boats were soon made of iron, they would be less noisy too.

In 1847, Cunard faced serious competition from an American company. Funded by the government, it was known as the United States Mail Steamship Company. However, it was named the Collins Line after its owner, New Yorker Edward Knight Collins, who had been running a packet service along the eastern coastline since the 1830s. Collins' fleet of four ships, the *Artic, Atlantic, Baltic,* and *Pacific,* nearly put Cunard out of business. Then disaster struck. In 1854, the *Artic* collided with another vessel and sank, killing nearly 300 on board. Two years later, the *Pacific* disappeared, presumably after hitting an iceberg, and taking with it a crew of 114 and 45 passengers. Both were equally damning for the business, but the *Arctic* tragedy was especially devastating for Collins, who lost his wife, two of his three children, his wife's brother, and his brother's wife in the wreck. Two years after the *Pacific* was lost in 1858, and only nine years after the American ships entered the fray, Congress ended the mail subsidy offer, Collins' contract was cut, and the service ended without paying a single dividend to its shareholders.

The *Arctic* disaster would continue to linger through the rest of the 19th century and early into the next as the most impactful and mournful event in the history of transatlantic steam. This was not

RMS *Mauretania*. The Library of Congress, part of the Detroit Publishing Co. [1907-1910].

only due to the great loss of life, but also to questions regarding disorder and discipline among both the crew and passengers in a time of crisis. These stories were eerily similar to those of a wreck that 58 years later would replace the *Arctic* as the worst and most definitive shipwreck on the Atlantic both in size and scope: the *Titanic.* Though smaller than the *Titanic,* one steamer, another Cunard liner, was to surpass them all, certainly in speed, but most imperatively in endurance and unquestionably in fortitude. She was the RMS *Mauretania.*

For those who write about the history of steamboat travel across the ocean, superlatives for the *Mauretania* can't come fast enough. "The *Mauretania* was the greatest steamship ever built," wrote author Stephen Fox, while another steamboat historian, John H. Shaum, Jr., went even further: "She is unquestionably, one of the most famous vessels of all time," he explained. Shaum, who had penned several books on the great Atlantic steamers, wrote the foreword to the latest printing of *Mauretania,* a full-length biography of the ship by Humfrey Jordan and published in 1936, shortly after the boat had been taken out of service. "Neither size nor speed could alone have given her fame," Shaum writes in the book, "that rested on something more secure and more intangible—on her individuality." The *Mauretania,* for its time, was indeed the fastest and most luxurious of all its predecessors. At 800 feet in length, she was nearly double the size of the *City of Paris,* a ship launched in 1889 that for two decades held the distinction of being the largest ship to cross the Atlantic. The *Mauretania* surpassed that in 1907. Since then, the only Cunard liner to come close to the *Mauretania* in size was her sister ship, the *Lusitania,* which was two feet shorter.

In 1909, the *Mauretania* set the record for the fastest westbound voyage across the Atlantic: 4 days, 10 hours, and 51 minutes, a standard that was set and held for 22 years. To compete with her, the White Star line commissioned three ships, including two, the *Olympic* and the *Britannic,* which were both slightly larger than the *Mauretania* in size, and the largest ship ever built, at 880 feet long, the *Titanic.* The White Star ships may have been bigger, but they were certainly not faster. In April of 1912, when the *Titanic* took its historic maiden voyage, no one was trying to set a time record. In fact, before the *Titanic* launched, her slogan was "great comfort, great space, and reasonable speed." She was also touted as the ship that was built "unsinkable." On the night of April 15, when the *Titanic* indeed did sink to the bottom of the Atlantic, the *Mauretania* was a day out of Queenstown and also bound for New York. Upon hearing the news of the disaster, she took a southward course, avoided the dreaded ice packs that doomed the *Titanic,* and had an uneventful trip across. This was perhaps the *Mauretania's* greatest asset, her ability to avoid trouble.

Whether the *Mauretania* is the "most famous" of all the ships, however, depends on your point of view. "Countless thousands of words have been written about her in a number of books, mostly by captains who commanded her 28-year life," reads Jordan's 1936 biography of the *Mauretania*. "On the sea she, as the phrase goes, made history; as a carrier of human freight, bringing men and women across the Atlantic to the building of those years, she was seldom divorced from, but very frequently gave assistance to, the shaping of events."

She also didn't sink, which may be why she isn't as well remembered as the other two big liners, the *Titanic* and *Lusitania,* both of which did. Regardless, by the time of her last voyage in the spring of 1934, she still averaged a respectable cruising speed of 24 knots. Her last transatlantic trip took place a year earlier, on September 26, when she sailed from New York to Southampton in just over five days. By this time, speed was no longer an important factor. The distance between the oceans had become considerably smaller again, thanks to several brave pioneers who chartered a different course, used a different method, and completed another seemingly impossible task. And it all begins on the most reliable steamship on the Atlantic, the grand lady, the RMS *Mauretania.*

6

One day,
I'm going to fly

◯ On May 4, 1919, two Englishmen, Arthur Whitten Brown and John Alcock, boarded the *Mauretania* and sailed from Southampton to Halifax, Canada, in the province of Nova Scotia. The five days at sea provided time for some reflection. For if they indeed made it back home to Great Britain, the two would have done what no man had done before them, would perhaps become national heroes, and would certainly be a whole lot richer. "I am coming back to claim you," Brown wrote to his fiancée Kathleen, clearly stating another reason why success promised personal rewards, too. Before leaving, he had kissed her goodbye and told her, "I have a hunch we are going to win."

The speed of the *Mauretania* served them well as they would arrive shortly before the SS *Glendevon,* a smaller ship designed to carry cargo. Aboard the *Glendevon* would be Alcock and Brown's transportation back to the shores of England, a modified British bomber, recently used in the Great War. Called a Vickers Vimy, it was named after its manufacturer, Vickers Limited, and the Battle of Vimy Ridge, a confrontation with the Germans by the Canadian Corps with the British Royal Flying Corps in the Nord-Pas-de-Calais region of France.

The Vimy biplane was a workhorse, reliable and designed for

long-range flights. But could it fly across the Atlantic nonstop? No one knew for sure, but Alcock and Brown, two former military men, were willing to find out. Their incentive was a cash prize offered by Britain's media mogul, Lord Northcliffe, who had been following the early stages of manned flight since the Wright Brothers. On April 1, 1913, Northcliffe announced in the *Daily Mail* that he would pay 10,000 British pounds to the first person to fly across the Atlantic. "Being myself a spectator of early attempts at flight," Northcliffe would later write about his lucrative offer, "I realized that what was wanted was tangible encouragement."

Similar contests for shorter flights and less prize money such as the crossing of the English Channel had already occurred, but the trip between the two continents was as much a challenge as it was a contest. Even the bravest of aviation pioneers knew it was nearly impossible to do. Aircraft were just simply not reliable enough to sustain such flights. "The prizes given by my journals," Northcliffe would explain, "were devised, therefore, to these two ends —to encourage the flying man and to interest the public." But this was in 1913, and the war intervened. Air warfare was now a part of the equation and efficiency in aircraft improved. Northcliffe's challenge was suspended at the outbreak of the war and then reinstated after it had ended. By then, engine design made it possible at least to consider a nonstop flight across the Atlantic as plausible, perhaps even attainable.

The war also had a profound impact on both Brown and Alcock. Born in Glasgow to American parents of English descent, Brown lived for a time in Manchester, England, where his father was sent to work as an engineer for the Westinghouse Electric and Manufacturing Company. Eventually, Brown would work for Westinghouse too, as an apprentice, where he inherited like his father the love for all things mechanical. He developed a keen interest in engines and became a proficient mechanic. He traveled across Europe by motorcycle and in 1913 went to St. Louis, Missouri, to study streetcar lighting and traffic systems. The war would put an end to his plans and hopes but not his travels. Although possessing American citizenship through his parents, Brown chose not to wait for the U.S. to enter the war and went back to Britain.

John Alcock. The Library of Congress, part of the Bain Collection [1915–1920].

In 1914, at the age of 28, Brown enlisted in the University and Public Schools Battalion, trained hard, earned a second lieutenant stripe, and found himself like others his age fighting for his life in the trenches. Through good fortune, as he described it, Brown was transferred to the Royal Flying Corps. "I had always longed to be in the air," he later wrote about his exploits with the Corps. He served as an observer checking for enemy artillery positions and confirming intelligence reports. Even as an observer, Brown went on combat missions, survived several crash landings, and eventually got captured by the Germans after a bullet pierced the fuel tank and shattered his left leg. Brown's pilot, a lieutenant by the name of Medilcott, somehow managed to get the plane on the ground. It was then they realized they were deep behind enemy lines. Brown, who in addition to his mangled leg also injured his hip and dislodged several teeth in the rough landing, bided his time and was eventually repatriated after 14 months of captivity.

It was during imprisonment that Brown, an avid reader, found time to study navigation. Brown does not explain or elaborate on why transatlantic flight interested him so, only that he had a love for aviation as a child and enjoyed being a part of the evolution of air combat in the Corps. The idea of flying long distances was the next logical or "third step," as he called it. His involvement in an actual transatlantic flight, however, was "entirely by chance." As Brown tells it, he was visiting the Vickers manufacturing plant in Weybridge and having a discussion about the Northcliffe challenge when another man walked in on the conversation. That man was Captain John William Alcock.

While Brown had no experience actually flying airplanes, Alcock most certainly did. Handsome, dashing, brave, and a bit reckless, Alcock possessed all the attributes associated with the early pioneers of flight. He also shared a name with an illustrious ancestor. John Alcock, one of Britain's revered historical figures from the 15th and 16th centuries, was a bishop who founded Jesus College in Cambridge. He eventually became Lord Chancellor of England under Henry VII, and one of the King's most trusted servants. Bishop Alcock was imprisoned once by Richard, Duke of Gloucester, for simply being an outspoken public figure, and could have been killed for such behavior, but persevered. Captain Alcock, like his ancestor, also had a reputation as "a fighter" who risked his life in other ways—in this case, flying an aircraft.

Born in 1892 in Old Trafford, Alcock lived a modest life, support-ed by his father, a horse coachman. By his teen years, Alcock had developed an interest in flight. In 1909—shortly after the Wright Brothers became famous—Alcock went to work for an engineer-ing firm in Manchester. There he found the owner, a man named Charles Fletcher, building an aircraft, a Farman-type biplane. He asked Alcock, who had mechanical experience, to help. When Al-cock realized the winner of a recent London-to-Manchester flight race was using a similar aircraft, he informed his father that it was an exact replica of the plane he was working on for Fletcher. "One day, I'm going to fly," Alcock announced. Three years later, he did.

Already an accomplished flyer when war broke out, Alcock was asked to train pilots for service in the Royal Air Force and even flew missions himself. This ended in September of 1917, when a plane he was guiding on a long-range bombing raid was shot at from the ground. Part of the plane's propeller was knocked off and struck a port auxiliary fuel tank, causing it to leak. Alcock and his two crewmembers were forced to land in the water just off Sul-va Bay on the Gallipoli Peninsula. They swam to shore, but were immediately surrounded by Turkish forces and reluctantly surren-dered. Alcock spent 13 months in relatively easy captivity, earned points for managing the rest of the detainees' activities like cook-ing and entertainment, and was eventually released. By the time he arrived back home in December of 1918, the war was over. "At last I was free to attack the big problem of crossing the Atlantic," he wrote. Less than five months later, both he and Brown were headed towards Halifax on the fastest steamship on the ocean. Their intent was to fly back to England.

By this time, the public was enthralled by flying machines and the men who flew them. Even Charles Lindbergh as a young boy caught the bug while marveling at a Wright flyer buzzing over the family farm in Minnesota. "Afterward, I remember lying in the grass and looking at the clouds and thinking how much fun it would be to fly up there among the clouds," he later wrote. That was in 1909, when Lindbergh's fame still lay nearly two decades away. But in 1911, nearly a decade before Alcock and Brown would even dream about flying over the Atlantic, one pilot became instantly famous for fearlessly doing what no man had been able to do or simply wasn't brave enough to try: the first transcontinental flight across the United States. While Cal Rodgers' name is lost among the more familiar aviation greats, his story is as remarkable as it is forgotten.

It starts with a man whose name is not unfamiliar: William Randolph Hearst. Said to be obsessed with aviation, Hearst, through his papers, also portrayed himself as a cheerleader for the American spirit. Hearst played on the nation's sensibilities to reclaim ownership of manned flight, something he thought the Wright Brothers compromised by going to France. Aviation was becoming the new frontier, like the railroad before it, and Hearst wanted a part. Personally, he pushed for more technology, supporting building better engines and more structurally sound designs. Sturdier machines and longer flight times, he insinuated, could be used for more practical purposes like transporting people or delivering the mail. He also hoped to sell a bunch of newspapers.

Through his morning daily, the *New York American,* Hearst offered an outrageous prize of $50,000 for any person "regardless of sex, nationality, race or residence" to fly across the United States in 30 days or less. The flyer could start on any coast at any time. There were no restrictions on stops along the way for repairs, but time was of the essence. In addition to the 30-day limit for the flight itself, the competitors would have a year to complete the journey beginning on October 10, 1910, or the deal was off.

Cal Rodgers was one of several upstart aviators who accepted the challenge. Tall, impeccably dressed, and always clamping a pickle-sized cigar between his teeth, the 31-year-old former football star at the University of Virginia had just received his pilot's license in August of 1911, a month before he and two others, Robert G. Fowler (an automobile racer turned aviator) and James "Jimmie" Ward (a former horse jockey), were set to compete for Hearst's prize. In September of that year, the race was on. Fowler would go first, starting in San Francisco and attempting an eastward route. Rodgers and Ward would set off from New York.

Jimmie Ward was only 19. While he had spunk, he lacked experience, especially in distance flying, though one could argue no one else had much experience in that either. Immediately after take-off, Ward lost direction and logged nearly 200 flight miles, mostly going in circles, before landing for the night in Patterson, New Jersey, just 21 miles from where he had started. Ward didn't seem to mind. He partied all night with newfound friends and missed an early take-off time the next day. Finally back in the air, it just got worse: engine troubles would force him down again.

Meanwhile, Fowler was having problems of his own. After a successful first day of traveling 179 miles between the snowy Sierras, his next day was quite different. Experiencing engine trouble from the start, the plane lost its rudder in mid-flight and Fowler crash-landed into a hillside near Colfax. Fowler was shaken and bruised, but otherwise fine. The plane, however, was not. It would take days, possibly weeks, before repairs could be made. Fowler waited patiently by his plane's side, still determined to give it a go. He would try three more times, but wind and snow impeded his progress each time. Finally, fighting a fierce 40-mile per-hour headwind which made his plane seem to stand still in the air, Fowler gave up.

On September 17, four days after Jimmie Ward, Rodgers took off from a horse track in Sheepshead Bay, Brooklyn. Considering the pitfalls faced by the other two pilots, no one gave him much of a chance. Bets were placed that he wouldn't make it beyond the Hudson River. Yet there was something about Rodgers and his Wright EX Flyer that was different from the rest of the competitors: The Vin Fiz.

Made by Armour, the massive meat and food packing company out of Chicago, the Vin Fiz was advertised as a "sparkling grape drink," actually more like syrup, that was mixed with other drinks to heighten the sweetness and flavor. Armour was looking for a way to market their product and decided a sponsorship of Rodgers' flight would be the perfect means. Rodgers, who had no financial support other than his own, eagerly accepted the offer. Instantly,

Cal Rodgers. The Library of Congress, part of the Bain Collection [November 1911].

Rodgers' plane had a name, "Vin Fiz Flyer," and Armour had a clever slogan, "The Drink Above All."

Ironically, one of the backers of the contest was the man who inspired manned flight in the first place, Wilbur Wright. "It is one of the few prizes an aviator can reasonably hope to win," he offered. "The man who makes it will be exceptional, physically and intellectually." Hearst also interjected praise on the potential victor. "The first aviator to drive an airplane over this route will live in history," his *New York American* blared.

For better or worse, that would be Cal Rodgers. Although he was the only pilot to complete the route, and the first to fly an air machine from one coast to the other, he completed the journey in 49 days, or 19 days more than the contest allowed. In addition, his flight ended on November 5, past the allotted year timeframe. Despite this, Rodgers was still a national hero. "At the end of 1911," historian Simon Winchester wrote, "Cal Rodgers had become the best-known, most celebrated man in America."

Rodgers' daily log tells an exhausting tale. There were so many delays, so many stops and starts, that by the time he reached the Mississippi River, not quite half way, in 32 days, Hearst's prize money had already slipped away. The flight was so marred with breakdowns and mishap that had it not been for the Vin Fiz sponsorship, it would have likely ended within days. Armour had a special three-car railway train that Rodgers trailed from above. This not only helped him directionally, but on the second day of flight when the plane wrecked shortly after takeoff, the train was there, loaded with spare parts, to put the busted machine back together again.

Rodgers was another matter. By the time the wheels touched down in Pasadena, he had suffered a broken leg, skin lesions on his arm, and a lacerated skull. Despite the setbacks, he cheerfully acknowledged the enthusiastic crowd of 20,000 or more, then flew his plane 14 more miles so he could wet the wheels in the Pacific surf and thereby truly claim an ocean-to-ocean voyage by air. He then boarded a train back to New York and was home in a mere six days.

Five months later, he was dead.

With his popularity waning, and hoping to recreate some of the old magic, on April 3, 1912, Rodgers returned to California, this time Long Beach, and stepped into the bucket seat of his Vin Fiz Flyer once again. He delighted the enthusiastic crowd with several aerial stunts before the plane suddenly nose-dived into knee-deep water. The impact ripped the plane into piercing wooden splinters. Rodgers' throat was slashed and his neck broken. He was killed instantly. Although the cause of the accident was listed as "unknown," many believe a bird strike did him in. "He was thirty-three years and three months, and he changed the face and nature of aviation forever," wrote Winchester.

Today, while Cal Rodgers' name comes up in books about the early history of aviation, his story is mostly a footnote. His legacy is stuck in the years between the Wright Brothers and Lindbergh's glorified solo flight across the Atlantic when the plane, rather than the man, took center stage. Sure, the brave pilots in the war and the daring aviators who flew the airmail routes every day get their just due, but it was the plane, its technology, improvement, size, and shape that dominated the culture of flight for decades. Eventually, when the planes' efficiency allowed, rich men like Hearst and Northcliffe would offer large cash rewards to challenge pilots to test their own grit and the machines' durability to conquer distance and speed.

Case in point: Alcock and Brown.

In 1919, when Alcock and Brown arrived in Newfoundland, they weren't alone. Several other hopeful aviators also came with the same aspirations. One team comprised of Freddie Raynham and Charles W.F. Morgan and another headed by an Australian named Harry Hawker, along with Lt. Commander Kenneth Mackenzie-Grieve, would leave before Alcock and Brown. Poor weather and impatience did them in. For Hawker and Mackenzie-Grieve, the first to leave, the trip ended only halfway to the destination. Engine problems forced them to abandon the attempt and crash-land the plane in the Atlantic. The two bobbed in the waves for nearly an hour aided by special water-tight suits before help arrived in the form of a Dutch steamer named the SS *Mary*, whose crew fortunately spotted the plane's flare through heavy fog. For a time, the fate of Hawker and Mackenzie-Grieve was unknown and many presumed they had perished.

Meanwhile, Alcock and Brown were searching for a desirable place to take off and more favorable weather. Even worse, they were waiting for the plane which had been delayed by days on the cargo ship. When the Vimy finally arrived, it was time to go. The news that Hawker and Mackenzie-Grieve were alive was reassuring, but it also meant they were out of the race for now. This only inspired Brown, who later wrote, "To Hawker and Grieve we owed particular thanks, in that we profited to a certain extent by what we learned from the cabled reports of their experience."

On Saturday, June 14, Alcock and Brown set off. The wind had been howling earlier in the day but soon calmed. "The conditions seemed propitious," Alcock wrote, "so Brown and I decided to 'chance our arms.'" After a slightly bumpy take-off, they climbed to a comfortable 1,000 feet and could see only water below. Sixteen hours later, they flew over land again. This time it was Ireland. Guided by the towers of a Marconi wireless station, the Vimy landed in a bog in Clifden, a picturesque castle town on the Owenglin River which flows into Clifden Bay. Although speed of the flight was not an issue (Northcliffe stipulated the flight be less than 72 hours), Alcock estimated that they completed the 1,960-mile journey by covering "over two miles in a minute," which Alcock later remarked, "was very good going in the circumstances." The official time, according to Brown, was 16 hours and 12 minutes.

Although the flight was tested by fog, rain, and even hail, the plane itself performed admirably. Sustaining flight without the engine breakdowns which doomed the other prospective teams, the Vimy held its course. "Neither figuratively nor literally," Alcock wrote about the stamina of the aircraft, "it did not let us down." The two occupants were equally up to the task. At one point, hampered by a faulty air-speed indicator, Alcock looked down to see the white-capped waves just below. "Too close to be comfortable," he later recalled. Flying out of the soup and seeing the horizon more clearly, he regained control, picked up speed, and climbed back to 7,000 feet. Even the landing was rough. Alcock spotted an open field near the wireless tower and decided to set it down, but the field turned out to be a swampy bog. After skidding for a stretch, the plane's wheels stuck in the mud and the nose jutted into the ground. Both men were violently thrown forward by the jolt but braced themselves enough to walk away unhurt.

Great Britain's King George immediately sent a telegram on his behalf to the two flyers: "His majesty wishes to communicate at once with these officers and to convey to them the King's warmest congratulations on the success of their splendid achievement." Northcliffe and the *Daily Mail* gladly awaited the arrival of the two British heroes so they could award the prize money. "We lurched as we walked," Brown described, relating the stiffness that resulted from sitting in a cramped cockpit for 17 hours. "I felt a keen sense of relief at being on land again," he added, "but this was coupled with a certain amount of dragging reaction from the tense mental concentration during the flight, so my mind sagged."

A week later, they were knighted by the King.

Eight years later, in 1927, a slim American pilot named Lindbergh made the first solo flight over the Atlantic, and the names of Alcock and Brown began to slip into obscurity. "The story of this historic flight has been shamefully neglected," British historian and acclaimed spy novelist Len Deighton wrote in 2008. He's right, of course, but perhaps "overtaken" might have been a better choice of wording in this case. Alcock and Brown were simply nudged out of the way by an industry of firsts, each one more celebrated than the next. "Adulation for the all-American hero Lindbergh so distracted from the achievement of Alcock and Brown," wrote biographer Brendan Lynch, "that many later credited him [Lindbergh] with the honor of the first non-stop crossing."

The modest but determined Lindbergh was also competing for a prize. New York hotelier Raymond Orteig challenged any pilot —or pilots, for that matter—to fly nonstop across the Atlantic, just like Alcock and Brown had, but with some stipulations. The trip must be between New York and Paris or back—no exceptions, he demanded. Figuring weight would be an issue, Lindbergh decided to do it alone. He built a plane to specifications, wedged in his

Ruth Elder. The San Diego Air and Space Museum archives, public domain.

long thin frame, and in less than two days became the most famous
person in the world.

Lindbergh's story, of course, is much more complex, but it's
worth noting that upon arriving in Paris, Lindbergh was gracious
enough to honor those who had preceded him. "Alcock and Brown
showed me the way," he said. Unfortunately, Alcock didn't live long
enough to hear Lindbergh's commendation. Less than a year after
he and Brown successfully flew across the Atlantic, Alcock was
dead, killed when a plane he was piloting over France lost control
and plummeted back down to Earth. He was 27.

While Lindbergh courageously endured the large crowds that
greeted his every move, even he, the most recognizable face on the
planet, wasn't immune to being pushed aside in the headlines. In
this case, it was by another brave—some would say reckless—pilot,
who for a brief and fleeting moment kept the world holding its
collective breath.

In the fall of 1927, while "Lucky Lindy" was on a victory tour,
Ruth Elder, a dental assistant from Lakeland, Florida, announced
that she too would attempt to make a transatlantic flight from New
York to Paris. "When Lindbergh reached Paris (in May), I made
up my mind that I would be the first woman to make the trip," the
23-year-old Elder said.

Immediately the press picked up on her intentions, even if they
were perceived as slightly ridiculous. "Men in the summer should
strive to equal Lindbergh. Women should stay at home," *The Irish
News* snidely advised. Even Lindbergh himself, without naming
names, warned against dangerous stunts without a purpose. But
Elder could not be ignored. Soon her picture and story were plas-
tered all over the newspapers.

Elder took flying lessons from an instructor named George Haldeman, and on Tuesday, October 11, 1927, only five months after
Lindbergh's historic flight, Elder and Haldeman took off from
New York's Roosevelt Field in a specially built Stinson 'Detroiter'
monoplane named *American Girl*. "Well here goes nothing, that
may turn up something," Elder thought to herself. They never
made it to Paris, at least not by plane. Thirty-six hours into the
flight and with over 2,000 miles logged, they flew directly into a

sleet storm and took on ice. The two pilots ditched the reserve fuel to lighten the load, but when an oil pipe burst, there was no other choice. The ocean would need to be their landing strip.

In the middle of the Atlantic, Captain Goos of the Dutch tanker *Barendrecht* noticed a plane in distress: "She came rapidly up to us and flying over the ship threw down two messages." One of the messages ended up on the deck of the ship. The inscription read: "How far are we from land and which way?" It was signed: Ruth Elder. Several minutes later, the plane landed in the water next to the ship. "Thank you very much," Elder said as they pulled her and Haldeman to safety. Soon enough, the press got a telegram from the missing *American Girl:* "We are safe," it read.

Afterwards, Elder embarked on a celebrity tour that melded into a mildly lucrative movie career. She flew in a few barnstorming shows and worked for mogul Howard Hughes, founder of Trans World Airlines, as his aviation secretary. Skeptics who felt Elder's flight was just a publicity stunt to promote her own self-interests may have felt vindicated by her success, but in perfect irony, even if that were the case, she also claimed victory.

For a short time at least, it can be argued that Ruth Elder was as well-known as Lindbergh. So why is she forgotten today? That can be explained by the fact that while Elder did try, and her story did make the front-page news, she also failed. Five years later, in 1932, another woman would fly across the Atlantic, do it solo like Lindbergh, and become instantly famous. Her name and legacy are soundly woven into the annals of American aviation history not just for her landmark accomplishments, but for the fascination that still exists today surrounding her mysterious disappearance. Her name, of course, is Amelia Earhart.

7

Nellie Bly,
watch over me

꙰ Despite these breakthroughs in solo flight, the idea of actually moving a large group of people long distances was another
matter. In 1919, the same year Alcock and Brown's Vimy successfully made it across the Atlantic, a 643-foot airship called the R34,
piloted by a British commander named Major George Herbert
Scott, made the first east-to-west ocean crossing and return trip
as well. Though large airships can be considered the direct descendants of the first balloons, one innovation enabled the dirigible (a
name derived from the Latin verb "dirigire," meaning "to direct")
to advance the idea of ballooning as a means of transport: the ability to power and steer it. Now large-scale balloons, some as long
as ocean liners, were not only going up, but forward too, driven
not just by the wind, but by engines and machines that could move
them in any direction.

Occurring only a month after the excitement of Alcock and
Brown's prize-winning flight, the R34 got lost in the mix of par-
ties, parades, and the King's knighting of the two British heroes.
Still, Alcock and Brown admitted that airships, not airplanes, were
the future of economical transport across the ocean. "For longer
distances," Brown wrote, "the airship has no competitor." Brown
used the German-made "Zeppelin"–named for its founder and
manufacturer Count Ferdinand von Zeppelin–as an example of

good navigation and transport. "Communications from two sep-
arate stations, which could be either land terminals or stationary
ships in the ocean, gives the direction of the transmitted wireless
waves, and signals to the dirigible its bearings," he continued. "It
may be deduced that in years to come, when the world's airways are
in general operation, heavier-than-air machines will bring freight
to the great airports, there to be transferred to dirigibles, and by
them carried to the earth's uttermost ends."

In 1928, a year after Lindbergh flew the *Spirit of St. Louis* into
history, a giant German airship named the *Graf Zeppelin* took
aboard 20 passengers and thus became the first transatlantic commercial flight. The trip was far from perfect. At one point, a portion of the outer skin was sheared off and had to be sewn back
together using blankets. Yet despite a few missteps, everyone was
quite pleased. The airship was considered relatively safe, surprisingly comfortable and—considering its size—fairly quick. It covered
the nearly 10,000 miles in 111 hours, far more time than a winged
craft could, but certainly faster by days than a ship.

Years later, in 1936, an American journalist named Dorothy Kilgallen boarded an even larger airship dubbed the *Hindenburg* and
marveled as the mighty craft swiftly passed over the tankers below.
"She dipped her colors as the shadow of the great ship slid over
her decks," Kilgallen pronounced. Of course, the name *Hindenburg* would soon be etched in memory as one of the most recognizable and frightful air disasters in history, but that would be a year
later, in 1937. On this particular trip, traveling from Lakehurst,
New Jersey, to Frankfort, Germany, Kilgallen described the landing in "record speed" and the flight "packed with thrills, adventure and suspense."

She was in fact touting her own exploits. On September 30, just
before the *Hindenburg* set off, Kilgallen's father, James, a New
York newspaperman, was among the well-wishers. "I waved goodbye as you started across the Atlantic on your dash around the
globe," he wrote. Indeed, the 23-year-old Kilgallen, also a writer
for the *New York Journal,* was on a mission to travel around the
world. She had decided to embark on the quest after reading about
two other reporters from rival newspapers who planned to "race

around the world." Both were men. Their motivation was inspired in part by the fact that several winged aircraft known as clippers, essentially flying boats and carrying mostly mail, were making voyages across the Pacific Ocean. A preview passenger flight would take off that year. The two reporters would make the inaugural flight the final leg of their journey.

Kilgallen wanted in. She went to her editor at the *Journal* and brought it up in conversation without actually asking the question directly. The editor, a man named Amster Spiro, hesitated at first, and then asked, "So you really want to go around the world?" Dorothy excitedly answered with another question: "When do you want me to start?"

Kilgallen, along with her two competitors, H.R. Elkins of the *New York World-Telegram* and Leo Kieran of the *New York Times,* all boarded the *Hindenburg* for the first and longest part of the trip. For Kilgallen, at least, the comparison to another female writer who also traveled around the world could not be ignored. "Nellie Bly did the world in 72 days," Kilgallen wrote, invoking the spirit of her predecessor, "but she wore a bustle and she didn't have airplanes." In fact, Kilgallen would use mostly airplanes and trains to move about. "I plan to take a plane from Frankfort to Rome, then go by motor or train to Brindisi, from there by plane to Hong Kong," she wrote, describing her itinerary to the readers of the *Journal.* Kilgallen played up every feeling, every nuance, and every grand new adventure. "I can't discover a new world," she wrote. "But I can discover the fastest way of getting around it." Through it all, she had a guiding spirit: "Nellie Bly, watch over me. You may be astonished at what you see—but watch, anyway."

Like Bly nearly 40 years earlier, Kilgallen thrilled the readers of the *Journal* with her daily dispatches and headlines: "Dorothy Speeding East, Athens, Next" and "Dorothy in Egypt; Bagdad Next."

One that caught everyone's attention was dated October 13 and read "Dorothy Faces Death." Her readers discovered that Dorothy survived a forced landing in the jungles of Indo-China where "tigers and great constrictor snakes lie in wait for little girls," she wrote. The pilot, having lost his way and running low on fuel, decided to land the small plane in the middle of a rice field in an area known to be filled with rebellious anti-Chinese government factions. "Thoughts of bandits, kidnappings, murders and revolutions sizzled in my head," related Kilgallen, who, along with the pilot, was able to escape unhurt. Hundreds of "chattering, nearly naked" natives surrounded the craft, and although they spoke no English, they were welcoming. "We waved our arms, made signs with our fingers, played 'handies,' and finally made them understand we were lost." After "a most terrifying, dizzy, breathless day of adventure," Dorothy boarded a commercial liner to Hong Kong and ended the "Death" story by recalling that her companion, the pilot, who was from Siam (now Thailand), told her that he learned how to fly an airplane in, of all places, St. Louis. The irony of that needed no more explanation.

On October 14, 14 days after she began, Kilgallen and Kieran arrived in Manila for the return trip to America. The *China Clipper* was late due to a typhoon warning. Kilgallen noted to her readers that Elkins was already on his way aboard another America-bound clipper named *Hawaiian*. Dorothy had gotten word he was refueling at Wake Island, nearly 3,000 miles ahead. "Oh, how I wish we could ride on the wings of a typhoon, or be catapulted across the ocean by some giant hand, so I could whizz by the proud Elkins," she wrote. The wait was excruciatingly long. "Will the spirit of Magellan, or Balboa, or someone, please come to the aid of a poor girl trying to get along and give that *China Clipper* a shove," she implored.

Finally, after five "agonizing" days, Kilgallen and Kieran stepped aboard the *China Clipper*, already filled with a dozen or so other journalists. "They can't stop us now," she declared. "I'll be the first woman to fly all the way across the Pacific." Indeed, she would be. So far, no woman had been allowed to take the clipper flights because there were no accommodations for "ladies" at some of the remote ocean landing sites, like Wake Island, where the plane was scheduled to stop for fuel. If the plane were to be delayed by weather or a mechanical breakdown, where would she stay? Pan American, the company that owned the *China Clipper*, at first refused the *Journal*'s request that a woman go on the flight, but relented when

Kilgallen insisted it was not an issue. "I'll even sleep standing up if I have to," she told them, "just as long as I can make that trip."

On October 24, 1936, Kilgallen was back on American soil. The clipper had done its job, making the nearly 8,000-mile-long journey from Manila to San Francisco in just five days. Dorothy cheerfully told her readers that while she was elated to be on schedule, her "hurry" did not compare to a young officer on board, a man named Francis Scott Key Lewis. Lewis was sweating out each stop in hopes that he would make his own wedding, scheduled for October 26. "The real reason for wanting to be back," she wrote admiringly.

In San Francisco, Kilgallen boarded another plane and before long was in Newark, New Jersey. "I'm back home–and my, but it seems good." Good, yes, but not perfect. Even though it was technically not a competition and no one would win a prize for finishing first, of the three journalists who went around the world, Dorothy was the second fastest. Kieran of the *Times,* her companion on the *China Clipper,* used another and presumably slower plane across the U.S., and finished third. As expected, Elkins had them all beat by taking the first available clipper hours before Kilgallen and Kieran arrived in Manila. It was a substantial and easy victory for the *World-Telegram* reporter, if anyone cared.

Dorothy was the star. While acknowledging the loss ("I came in second") and congratulating her compatriots' efforts ("Both grand fellows!"), Kilgallen regaled her readers by highlighting her achievements. She was, after all, not only the first woman to fly over the Pacific Ocean, but as she discovered upon her return, the fastest person to make the 5,000-mile-plus trip from Honolulu to New York in 34 hours and 25 minutes. The final time for the whole journey was 24 days, 12 hours, and 51 minutes, "[figuring] the time I left the city room at the *New York Evening Journal* until I checked back in there yesterday morning," she wrote in her second-to-last dispatch. "This is almost three times as fast as Nellie Bly. But, of course, I had available the modern speed methods of transportation."

Her final article was published in the *Journal* on October 26, 1936, and titled "GLAD TO SEE NEW YORK AGAIN". She wrapped up the adventure by giving her home city an advertising slogan for the ages: "I remember leaving New York, and coming back to it. Because no matter how far you go, or how much you see, New York is always waiting for you, calling you back, always the friendliest, always the best, always home." But it wasn't just Kilgallen's charm that made her instantly famous: being the only female on the trip seemed to ramp up the excitement as well. Her firsthand accounts were not only descriptive, but personal. They captured both a city's heart and a nation's attention. On the day she arrived back in New York City, Kilgallen received a letter that was postmarked from Washington, D.C.:

> *Dear Miss Kilgallen:*
>
> *I have been so interested in your flight around the world with the men, and even though I am sure you are disappointed in not being the first to arrive, I wanted to tell you that I was rather pleased to have a woman go! It took a good deal of pluck and it must have held a good many thrills.*
>
> *With congratulations and good wishes I am*
> *Very sincerely yours,*
> *Eleanor Roosevelt*

The First Lady's affirmation was no fluke. Nearly a decade-and-a-half after the ratification of the 19th amendment in 1919, Dorothy Kilgallen stood as an example of a woman who defied the odds and succeeded in a world largely influenced by men. While Nellie Bly was the epitome of perseverance, especially in the male-dominated world of journalism, Kilgallen's métier was breaking the social taboos of women that still existed in the workplace. Beyond fighting for the right to vote, the nearly century-long equality movement was striving to break down the barriers that separated men from women in status and acceptance.

With that kind of progressive thinking in the forefront, and in a completely different manner than Bly or Kilgallen would, one woman named Victoria Woodhull sought to change an institution.

Woodhull was somewhat of an enigma in the women's rights movement. She dabbled in spiritualistic medicine and séances and expressed her support for "free love" by claiming the right even as a married woman to take as many lovers as she pleased. Together with her equally spirited sister Tennessee Claflin, Woodhull set out to prove that women like herself had every right to speak out and be heard. Although controversial, Woodhull would make a statement by doing something no woman had dared to do before her. In her quest to succeed, she also became associated with two men, each persuasive in his own right. One was George Francis Train. His connection to Woodhull is based on circumstance and conviction. The other is Cornelius Vanderbilt, and his relationship to Woodhull and her sister proved more personal. That contemptuous tale lies ahead. First, in regards to Train's story...

On May 1, 1893, the World's Columbian Exposition opened in Chicago to great excitement along the shoreline of Lake Michigan. It was a grand affair set against a backdrop of statues, fountains, and a towering passenger-carrying wheel that was named after the person who conceived it: George Washington Ferris. Adding to the splendor of the Fair were large, ornate-looking buildings comprised mostly of plain stucco and given the distinctive, though unofficial, moniker of the "White City." At night, the "White City" was gloriously illuminated by electricity, thanks to Tesla's new alternating-current induction motor. The Fair had been planned for several years, and the city showed its appreciation that day: an estimated quarter of million people packed the grounds.

Despite all the pomp and grandeur surrounding opening day, however, the Fair itself got off to a slow start. The Ferris Wheel was not quite finished yet and some of the elaborate structures were still under construction. The next day, only 10,000 people showed up.

Train, who was looking to resurrect his own status as a leader of the people, was asked to come to Chicago and help rescue it. That, at least, is how he described it. With characteristic braggadocio, Train proclaimed that he and only he had the wherewithal to give the Fair a boost. He planned to increase attendance by literally electrifying the crowds with his so-called "psychic energy." Dressed in an all-white suit, red belt, and Turkish fez hat, Train paraded around the grounds pretending to reach out his hands in a friendly gesture only to snatch them away in jest, lest he give away

NELLIE BLY, WATCH OVER ME   193

the potency of his electrical powers. It was silly and odd, but Train played it to the hilt. "Chicago built the Fair," he boldly proclaimed. "I am here to save it and I'll be hanged if I haven't."

The drawing power of Train's antics is difficult to gauge. By then he had twice run for president of the United States and thrice circled the globe. This alone would justify his attendance, but Train was Train, and his sincerity was always in question. "He was one of the most famous men of his day," one author wrote. "But no one knows quite why." Another writer and an acquaintance of Train's was more forthright: "His kindness of heart was unquestionable, but his humanity was never to fore, if he had any."

In Chicago, the boldness of Train's appearance at the Fair had a much deeper connotation for those who had lived through the city's darkest day, some 22 years before. The Fair was a chance to show the world that the "city of big shoulders," as Carl Sandburg would later describe it, had risen from the ashes of destruction and despair, survived, and prospered. Train viewed it differently.

He was in Chicago on the day it almost fell. Now he was back to save it again.

Great Chicago Fire aftermath. The Library of Congress, photo of painted cyclorama by G.M. Watson [1871].

Part IV

⤢ By the time John "Jex" Bardwell arrived, the fires were out, but the smoldering continued. It continued not just in the streets, where ashen piles of wood and stone were all that remained where buildings once stood. It continued in the attitude of the people of this working city, who wondered how so much could change in so little time.

It was October 8, 1871, and Bardwell, along with the rest of the nation, was reacting to the news that the largest metropolis in the Midwest, the City of Chicago, the Garden City, the Gem of the Prairie, had burnt to the ground. Or at least a good portion of it.

Bardwell was a photographer on a mission. Actually, he came on a commission. The Michigan Central Railroad who had a rail line used to transport cattle to the stockyards wanted to record the damage to their tracks. They knew "Jex" Bardwell from Detroit had a camera, so they sent a telegram asking for his help.

Bardwell immediately packed up his bulky equipment, boarded the next train, and steamed his way west. Taking photos of rail cars and tracks destroyed by the fire was only part of it. Bardwell wanted to capture a moment in time. Hundreds of buildings had been destroyed, and Bardwell created a visual record of it all. "Here and there a tall jagged piece of wall limps its form above the chaotic mass of brick and stone," one observer noted, surveying the damage. Bardwell stood before each street corner and held the shutter of his camera box open just long enough to sear another image onto a negative.

One of Bardwell's most famous pictures of the Great Chicago Fire was taken at the corner of Madison and Clark, where a grand meeting place known as Farwell Hall once proudly stood. Only the day before, the Hall had been filled to capacity to hear a man speak. Now just the front stood with the side and back walls destroyed.

When Bardwell took a photo of what was left of Farwell Hall, he was unaware that city officials were looking for the man who gave the speech just hours before the flames took hold. They wanted to ask him a few questions, for they had heard he said something that raised a few eyebrows.

He had predicted the city was doomed.

1
My individual independence

In 1868, at the age of 74, Cornelius Vanderbilt had recently lost his wife and youngest son George, a Civil War veteran, to illness. Ailing himself, Vanderbilt sought out psychics and mediums to guide him through the grief and despair. It was for this reason that Vanderbilt's dozen or so children questioned his sanity during the last years of his life and held heated debates after his death to determine who had claim to the family fortune. While he was still alive, however, Vanderbilt looked to ease his suffering, both physically and mentally, and so he turned to Victoria Woodhull.

It's unclear exactly how the two met. Several stories emerge that involve Vanderbilt's reliance on another spiritualist's "prescription" that did him some good. Vanderbilt may have seen Woodhull's advertisement in his neighborhood and, since she'd opened a shop near his estate, sought her out. More likely, she came to him. Recently widowed and grieving over a lost son, Vanderbilt could have been easy prey for an enchanting mender like Woodhull and her equally alluring sister, Tennessee.

Since much of the traditional medicine and remedies being administered at the time, such as mercury for syphilis, were akin to torture, Woodhull and her sister advertised their services as being less painful and more compassionate. They also communicated with the dead. In the eyes of many, including many women, they

were con artists. Some men, however, saw them quite differently.
To them, the sisters were healers who made the old and forsaken
feel content and young again. They were also both quite strikingly good-looking. They charged $25 just to be seen, and it was no
secret that they catered to a more affluent male clientele.

The sisters offered Vanderbilt their services, and some believe
even more, as rumors of an affair with the 24-year-old Claflin
emerged. In return, Vanderbilt gave the sisters stock tips. In 1869,
when two Wall Street shysters made a foiled attempt to corner the
gold market, Victoria Woodhull, using sound advice from Vanderbilt, came out a self-proclaimed "winner." In fact, she pocketed
enough cash that in February of 1870, she and her sister opened
up their own brokerage firm on Wall Street, Woodhull, Claflin,
Co., the first ever run exclusively by two women.

The other banking firms questioned who was really behind this
sudden venture. Although they were "just as capable of making
a living as a man," the sisters weren't shy about revealing that
Vanderbilt, whom they and others called "the Commodore," was
a partner in the firm. "If not the full partner in the firm," the
New York Herald reported, adding, "a rather free use has been
made of the name of the veteran Commodore Vanderbilt as aid-
er and abettor." Vanderbilt never publicly disclosed that he had
endorsed or joined the firm, only that he was quite fond of both
women. Many assumed that he was madly in love with the seduc-
tive Claflin. "Impressed with the sister's intelligence, allure and
forthrightness, he put their money in the stock market, and made
a small fortune for them," wrote Vanderbilt biographer T.J. Stiles.
"But their notoriety, and his discomfort, would grow."

Before long, and for several reasons, their relationship became
strained. For one, Vanderbilt remarried, either ending or quiet-
ing the affair talk. Lawsuits followed as the firm's poor account-
ing began to reveal bad lending practices. "I do not recollect of
any authority given by me to them to use my name in their business," Vanderbilt angrily refuted when called to testify on behalf
of one duped investor's case. In return, the sisters, especially Victoria, shot back. She accused Vanderbilt of being dishonest and his
words deceitful. Her biting criticism leveled at the Commodore

was manifested on the lecture circuit and in a newspaper called the *Woodhull & Claflin Weekly,* a clever creation by the sisters to boost Woodhull's political aspirations and defend their own actions. It struck a nerve. Woodhull became an unsuspecting and emerging figure in an already influential movement.

Soon, she would be its star witness.

When the 15th Amendment passed in 1870, women were empowered to test its somewhat ambiguous language: "The right of the citizens of the United States to vote shall not be denied or abridged by the United States or by any State on account of race, color, or previous condition." Of course, this meant men, with the only difference being black men, who were now allowed to vote. The word "citizens," women protested, had no gender distinction, an argument also made when the 14th Amendment was passed making ex-slaves citizens of the United States. The men who drafted the 14th Amendment made their intentions steadfastly clear by including the word "male" when it came to voting rights. Never before had such a term been used in the Constitution and many vocal abolitionists denounced it. The First Amendment, they argued, gave every "citizen" the right to free speech and press, but voting was different. The Constitution allowed for the individual states to define who could vote.

Then the Civil War came and went. It established a more federal role in government and more power to enact and mandate laws that overruled states' rights, like the 13th Amendment which banned slavery nationwide. When the 14th Amendment was drafted, giving the federal government alone the right to define who could vote, its writers felt the need to include the distinction "male" to its wording. It created, as everyone soon found out, a conundrum. For the next two years, the American Equal Rights Association, formerly the American Anti-Slavery Society, argued against ever using that word in the Constitution again. They succeeded in the 15th Amendment, only to create more confusion. There was no gender restriction at all, and women's rights activists sought to exploit it.

As they had tried unsuccessfully before, in 1872, on the day of the presidential election, many women marched to the polls in their respective states and demanded to vote. They were turned down. In Rochester, New York, however, some 15 women, including Susan B. Anthony, voted and were subsequently arrested. The women had tried to use the 15th Amendment as a loophole. The word "citizen" was clearly unambiguous and meant all taxpaying citizens, including women, who paid taxes too. Elsewhere in the text, only nouns like "citizens" or "peoples" were used, making an even stronger argument for inclusion. It was showy and effective but mostly mocked by men. When Anthony was arrested for voting, she was fined $100 but refused to pay, hoping her resistance would bring even more awareness to the cause. Instead, the judge ignored the fine and let her go. The irony of that day, however, was in the election itself. Among the candidates running for president was a woman: Victoria Woodhull.

Woodhull's announcement that she was a candidate for president came just six weeks after the opening of the Wall Street firm, and shortly after a visit by Anthony, who praised the sisters for their ingenuity and willingness to challenge a man's world. "Instead of making shirts for fifty cents each (one per day) for a living, these two ladies (for they are ladies) determined to use their brains, their energy, and their knowledge of business to earn them a livelihood," Anthony noted, although admitting they were still uphill climbers. "Wall Street has been so exclusively monopolized by men that it has not yet got over a bad habit of staring at a passing woman."

Whether Woodhull and her sister intended to see the Wall Street experiment through or just to use it as a springboard for more money and fame is debatable. An endorsement by Anthony, the leading figure of the women's rights campaign, was a good start. Woodhull nudged her way into the movement with a bold proclamation. "While others of my sex devoted themselves to a crusade against the laws that shackle the women of the country, I asserted my individual independence," she wrote in a letter to the New York papers, explaining that the Constitution, while not allowing women to vote, says nothing about a woman not being able to run for office. "I therefore claim the right to speak to the un-enfranchised woman of the country," she noted.

Woodhull's intentions were surprising. She had never even hinted at such a move, nor was she "already in the political arena," as she boldly proclaimed. However, in the context of an established pattern of ambitious and fulfilled desires, it was not an unusual one for the former healer. Furthermore, her campaign was not without precedent: In 1866, Anthony's predecessor, Elizabeth Cady Stanton, unsuccessfully ran for Congress in her New York district, picking up just 24 of 12,000 votes total. Woodhull's candidacy would differ from Stanton's and in the end prove highly controversial, as her past would suggest. Whether she could actually win remained another matter, but it certainly got everyone's attention. "She lit oratorical flames, created an Equal Rights Party, and held a convention to nominate Frederick Douglass for vice-president, despite his flat out refusal of this or any honor," wrote Doris Weatherford in *A History of the American Suffrage Movement.*

The abolitionist leader Douglass was generally appalled by the nomination. While he fought for the rights of all women, Douglass found Woodhull too radical, too outspoken, and too controversial to be President of the United States. Her support for "free love"– a woman's right to openly practice such sexual freedoms as having multiple partners irrespective of marriage–was a hot-button issue. Hypocrisy was her defense. If men can preach against it but then secretly do it, women should be afforded the same right without public ridicule or scorn. After all, who was to judge the morality of taking several lovers? By taking a stance, she was also using "free love" as a matter of self-defense. Woodhull, herself, was attacked for having too many men under one household. These included her former husband, Canning Woodhull, an alcoholic whom she took care of like a child, and her current husband, Colonel James Harvey Blood, a Civil War officer, who may have illegally married Woodhull while she was still legally bonded to her first husband. Blood and Woodhull at some point divorced and then remarried, although they never stopped living together.

All this marriage and remarriage and communal living was perceived as an assault against the laws of conventional marriage, and many believed that Woodhull should be punished for it. Instead, Woodhull cleverly turned the tables, advocating the practice of

Victoria Woodhull. Harvard Art Museums/Fogg Museum, Historical Photographs and Special Visual Collections department, Fine Arts Library, photographed by Bradley and Rulofson, public domain.

"free love," and silencing her critics with forthrightness and com-
passion: "My opinions and principles are subjects of just criticism.
I put myself before the public voluntarily. I know full well that the
public will criticize me, and my motives and actions, in their own
way in their own time. I accept the position." Eventually her open-
ness led her to trouble with the law. In 1872, shortly before the presidential election, both Woodhull and Claflin were arrested and
charged with obscenity and libel. They were accused of besmirch-
ing the image of two "honorable" men in their weekly newspaper.
One man, named Luther Challis, a Wall Street investor, was a rapist, the sisters claimed. The other, Henry Ward Beecher, a well-
known preacher and critic of Woodhull, was having numerous
adulterous affairs. These included one with the wife of Woodhull's
friend, Theodore Tilton, another free love advocate and supporter
of women's rights. Beecher's affairs did not appall Woodhull, for
as she explained they were "nobody's business," but his apparent
hypocrisy did.

The charge against Challis was even more disturbing. During a
large ball at the Academy of Music in Baltimore, Claflin had witnessed Challis and a friend serve two young girls alcohol and then
seduce them. "You may be sure I followed the girls up and got the
history of their connection with the men," she wrote in the *Woodhull & Claflin Weekly.* Her language in the article, which included
graphic descriptions and observations, was stark and shocking.

When the paper hit the newsstands in October of 1827, rumors
of blackmail by the sisters had already surfaced. Woodhull and
Claflin denied obtaining or demanding any money from Challis
or Beecher; they only wanted justice. This wasn't enough for some
of their more outspoken critics, among them Anthony Comstock,
a well-known public morals advocate who filed a federal warrant
charging the sisters with sending obscene content through the U.S.
mail system. It was convoluted, but legal. Comstock himself had
cleverly ordered two associates to send the paper, thereby initiating the charge. The two sisters were arrested and sent to jail.

Comstock's charge was deceiving, but in his mind, clearly warranted. He intended to put the sisters and their newspaper out of
business. The accused rapist Challis, on the other hand, lawyered

up and charged the sisters with libel. Perhaps most telling was the preacher and suspected womanizer, Beecher, who remained mostly silent about the sisters' accusations, leaving many of his parishioners and ardent followers to scratch their heads.

One man who was clearly on the side of the sisters' plight and outraged at their arrest was George Francis Train.

Like Vanderbilt, Train admired the sisters, but for vastly different reasons. Although Train barely knew them personally, he had followed their exploits in the paper. He thought they had been wronged, especially concerning the charge of obscenity. Train was no stranger to women's rights. In 1866, around the time the suffragists were fighting for equal representation and Douglass was doing the same for freed slaves, Train helped Susan B. Anthony fund a newspaper of her own called *The Revolution*. It was a strange match. Anthony defended their association, but others, like William Lloyd Garrison, another abolitionist leader, chastised her for it. Garrison called Train a racist—which, based on Train's rhetoric at the time, wasn't entirely untrue.

Train and Anthony stumped together in Kansas, rousing crowds with their speeches and supporting the referendum that women should have just as much right to vote as black men. In the end, it didn't work. They lost the vote, but gained a sizable enough number of white men to their cause that Anthony claimed the loss as a victory for the movement. She gave Train credit for it even though their opinions regarding enfranchising black men differed. Still, Anthony saw the outcome as a positive. "The result was a respectable democratic vote in favor of women suffrage," she later recalled. Train's motives, as with everything else that he did or said, were harshly criticized. "He is as destitute of principle as he is of sense," wrote Garrison in a scathing letter to Anthony in January of 1868, "and is fast gravitating toward a lunatic asylum."

Train seemed to feed off the negativity. He was, after all, a candidate for President of the United States in 1868, and any publicity was good publicity. He wrote and published an epigram that compared himself to other notable history figures:

Columbus was mad as the Spanish Queen,

To cross the ocean before the age of steam.
Gallelio [sic] was mad above the Earth and Sun,
Almost as mad as Washington.
Franklin was mad when he drew at sight,
The lightning from Heaven with a kite;
Morse was mad when he did aspire
To make it talk with iron wire

Train's speeches were just as flamboyantly over the top. Even those who thought he was slightly off-kilter couldn't argue his hold on an audience. "In all seriousness," wrote A.C. Edmund, an admitted Train critic, "Mr. Train is a born orator. He sways men." When the 1868 presidential elections were over and the people overwhelmingly elected its first Civil War general, Train set his sights on 1872 and another chance to defeat the now incumbent President, Ulysses S. Grant. This time, he wasn't the only outsider in the race; there happened to be a woman running, too.

While Victoria Woodhull's campaign may have been more for show, Train actually thought he had a chance to win. "It seemed to me that, with the effect I have upon people in my speeches and in personal contact, and with the great achievements in behalf of the progress of the world, especially with regard to the development of this country, I should succeed," he wrote. Yet his methods seem indeed mad. He charged admission fees for people to listen to his campaign speeches. He proclaimed he was running for "Dictator of the United States," not President. He even promised—likely in jest, but with Train it is hard to tell—that he would hang all those who disagreed with him. To further his own popularity and to establish a connection with the advancement of travel across the United States and beyond, he circumnavigated the globe in 80 days. None of it mattered.

When Election Day hit on November 5, 1872, Train, like his counterpart Victoria Woodhull, was in jail.

Just days before the polls opened, Train was delivering a speech on Wall Street when he was handed a newspaper proclaiming Woodhull and her sister were arrested on obscenity charges. Immediately, Train sprang to their defense. He marched down to the Ludlow

Street jail where the two women were being held and told them personally that their words were "grand" and their "truths were eternal." He proceeded to write in charcoal on the jail cell's walls words of condemnation against their incarceration. He told them he would fight for their rights, and did so by publishing "erotic excerpts" from the Bible in his own newspaper. "Every verse I used," he proclaimed, "was worse than anything published by these women." Train was arrested for obscenity, the same charges he was accusing others of wrongfully initiating upon the sisters.

The presidential election came and went. Grant won again, but not as easily this time. If there were any votes for Train, they were not recorded. Woodhull may have picked up some support, but even Anthony, who symbolically cast a ballot and was arrested for it, voted for the Democratic candidate Horace Greeley.

A month later, Woodhull and her sister were freed from prison. Four years after, Woodhull would make good on a promise to start a new life. First, she divorced her second husband, Colonel Blood. Then, in 1877, upon receiving a considerable sum of money from William Henry Vanderbilt, the executor of his late father Cornelius Vanderbilt's large estate, she left for England. There she married a rich banker, made a few public appearances, and retired to a mostly quiet life in the English countryside.

Train didn't go away so quietly. After the elections, and still locked up in New York's notorious Tombs, Train went on a tirade. Escalating his need to be "dictator," he reiterated his intentions to hang the "criminals and thieves," including newspaper editors and even members of Congress whom he considered to be corrupt. It was in essence a parting shot. Upon his release from the Tombs, Train sailed to England and eventually Germany to be with his wife and two sons, who were studying in Frankfurt.

A year before he left, however, Train had another curious episode where his judgment (as well as his sanity) was questioned. It was the first instance—in print at least—that Train would be accused of being a "certifiable lunatic," something he would deny for the rest of his life.

More I cannot say;
more I dare not utter

On the morning of October 8, 1871, word spread across the nation that Chicago, the largest city in the Midwest, had been ravaged by fire. "Thousands of citizens witness the grand and awful illumination of the terribly destructive conflagration last night," the *Chicago Tribune* reported that day. The news, while shocking, also had a paradoxical ending. A consistent rainfall finally stopped the blaze from spreading and, in the process, stopped a long, warm dry spell too. Immediately city officials attempted to determine the cause of the fire. They knew approximately where it had started; possibly even the street, but why did it start and who was responsible? In the meantime, photographers came from all over the country, set up their tripods, opened their box shutters, and recorded the vast devastation.

John "Jex" Bardwell was one.

Born in London in 1824, Bardwell came to America with his family and settled in Ann Arbor, Michigan. There he trained to be a brewer and distiller, work which pleased him—and others too —but offered no personal rewards. In 1841, after his father's death, Bardwell returned to London to settle affairs. It is there where he learned photography.

Back in Michigan at the outset of the Civil War, Bardwell turned his camera on the troops at Fort Wayne in Detroit as they trained for battle. His work was getting noticed, not just in his hometown, but across the nation. Then he received a telegram sent to his studio from the Michigan Central Railroad, who ran a line in Chicago used to transport cattle to the stockyards. The rail yard had been ravaged by fire and they wanted to record the heat damage to their tracks. "Send for Bardwell," the telegram read.

In addition to the rail lines, Bardwell took photos of the decimated buildings. Many prominent structures were destroyed beyond repair, but the scenery, while ghastly, had an eerie stillness to it. One of Bardwell's most striking photographs is the ornate facade of a meeting place now reduced to mostly debris. It once housed a hotel, several stores, meeting rooms, and a grand hall, the largest in Chicago at the time. The Hall was named after John V. Farwell, a local merchant and philanthropist, who was one of the first contributors to the Young Men's Christian Association, also known as the YMCA.

Farwell Hall sat on a full city block, flanked by Washington and Madison on one side and Clark and LaSalle on the other. For the purposes of the YMCA, it contained a library and a gymnasium and 45 small rooms that occupied the upper floors above the main floor, which housed the great hall. The hall's grand entrance was on Madison Street. Bardwell's photograph shows just the entrance with only a part of an exterior wall still standing. Behind it there is nothing left, just a hollow space occupied by stone rubble. In the history of the Great Chicago Fire, Farwell Hall is mentioned in several instances as being the building that spread the flames to the nearby Cook County Courthouse, jail, and city hall offices, all completely destroyed as well. Its significance is also infamously linked to the speech of George Francis Train.

Shortly after returning from his trip around the world, Train went on a whirlwind speaking tour in support of his presidential bid. His rantings were crowd pleasers, as much out of curiosity's sake as for their content. Still, Train was energized by the crowds and seemed to get more radical and rankled at each stop. On the evening of October 7, 1871, Train found himself in Chicago's Farwell Hall in front of a packed audience. His speech, while not transcribed, was recalled by witnesses who repeated what they had heard from the podium that night. "This is the last public address that will be delivered within these walls," Train told the crowd. "A terrible calamity is impending over the city of Chicago. More I cannot say; more I dare not utter."

Train's flair for the dramatic was not lost on the audience. As shocking as those words seemed to be, listeners mostly dismissed the threat. Train had said or written similar accusations against Chicago, the "city of doomed sin" as he called it, but none so brazen as to predict a doomsday scenario for its people. The next day, as if on cue, the city was consumed by fire.

Train's threatening prophecy did not resonate until after the awful calamity was over. When the flames finally settled some 27 hours after they had begun, the damage was unnerving: numerous buildings had been destroyed, hundreds had been left homeless, and 300 people were killed. Rumors began circulating as fast as the blaze itself. Train's past had come back to haunt him. Even his trip around the world, when he was briefly jailed for standing up for the rights of embattled labor workers and communist sympathizers in France, was called into question.

The *Chicago Times* was the first to report Train's speech and incriminating words, claiming he was part of a fringe revolutionary group Societe Internationale based in Paris with off-shoot chapters around the world, including Chicago. The *Times* even published a confession, said to be by an exiled Paris communard who claimed to have set the fire to "humble the men who waxed rich at the expense of the poor."

Not everyone agreed. The other newspaper in town, the *Chicago Evening Journal,* was more measured in its approach. It debunked the claims of collusion between Train and the Paris group and blasted the rival *Times* for concocting a communist plot against the city. Still, Train had some explaining to do. He said his prediction was in response to shifty government policies that left a neglected city and its crumbling infrastructure prone to disaster –either by fire or flood. The timing, he said, was purely coincidental. Train then threatened to sue the offending newspaper for defamation unless it retracted the charges.

In his definitive book about the Great Chicago Fire published in 1958, author Robert Cromie writes about Train as a starting point of the narrative. "It is likely that his prediction was designed merely to grip the attention of a restless Saturday night audience," Cromie speculates, "yet plain common sense and the most casual observer could have told him that if Chicago was indeed in danger, that danger was fire." Cromie's point was this: Chicago, just by virtue of being a city of industry, was a tinderbox ready to ignite. "It might be said, with considerable justice," he wrote, "that Chicago specialized in the production, handling, and storage of combustible goods." Weather conditions played a role as well: "The city was parched and dehydrated, and the first week of October was unusually warm for the season." Cromie seems to suggest that Train should have been given credit for being a keen forecaster, not a lunatic, as others labeled him, but admits, "The prophet's hindsight was less precise than his foresight."

Using Chicago's plight as fodder, Train continued his speaking tour. "The concentrated energy of 20 years of organized labor and capital was destroyed in 20 hours," he said, fueling the flames of controversy even more. A week later, on October 16, in Louisville, Kentucky, Train was asked directly if he had really foretold the city's doom. "Yes," he bluntly answered, but added, "Many persons attribute to me simply an impulsiveness, and an impressibility, as though I was some erratic comet, rushing madly throughout space, emitting coruscations of fanciful colored sparks, without system, rule or definite object." In defense, he claimed to be "a close, analytical observer of passing events, applying the crucible of truth to every new matter or subject presented to my mind or senses." Train's sanity aside, the fire itself was befuddling. "Who can explain the strange fact that the stone and mortar habitations on the North Side are heaps of rubbish while Ogden's wooden mansion, although surrounded by a sheet of fire, has not even the paint thereon blistered?" Train pointed out.

The "Ogden" he mentions is Mahlon D. Ogden, a successful attorney and judge, and the younger brother of William B. Ogden, Chicago's first elected mayor in 1837. Train had asked, as others certainly did, why his residence was spared while every single

"Great Chicago Fire 1871". The Library of Congress, Stereograph Cards Collection [1871].

house near it was completely destroyed. "Everything is reversed. Right is wrong; white became black; and topside is bottom's up," Train said. "How explain the strange infatuation of the Chicago shoddy lords building palaces of limestone that burned like kindle wood?" Train's motivation was obviously political, but the truth was the truth. Ogden's mansion was indeed the only residence left untouched in the fire's destructive path, an area that stretched for several miles between the Chicago River and Lincoln Park.

Had it been deliberately saved? Train asked. Outside of a few ardent Train supporters, most Chicagoans simply chalked it up to sheer coincidence or plain luck. Good planning may have been the real reason, as wet carpets were reportedly placed along the home's base. The sparks, apparently, amazingly danced around it.

Train's observance, while substantial, did not directly include the other more well-known Ogden, Mahlon's influential brother and former mayor, who wasn't so lucky. William B. Ogden lost just about everything in the blaze, including his lavish estate, Ogden Grove, the first house in Chicago designed by an architect. The Grove sat on a full city block surrounded by a mass of trees and flanked by a conservatory filled with fruits and flowers.

Ogden, like Train, became wealthy in real estate. He bought government land meant for new settlers, sometimes for other buyers, and held it until it appreciated. The property doubled and sometimes tripled in value. "I purchased in 1845, property for $15,000 which, twenty years thereafter, in 1865, was worth ten millions of dollars," he wrote in his notebook. The practice came under widespread criticism, but there was nothing illegal about it. "When you are dealing with Chicago property the proper way is to go in for all that you can get and then go with your business and forget about it. It will take care of itself," Ogden said.

Ogden wasted no time in creating a transportation and industrial hub on the banks of Lake Michigan. He contracted the construction of the I&M Canal and was instrumental in the success of Chicago's first rail line, the Galena Railroad, a planned route from the Chicago Union Railroad to Galena, Illinois, located on the far northwest tip of the state, close to the Mississippi River. Ogden earned capital by recruiting farmers along the route to buy stock subscriptions. He was convinced this new railroad idea would be an unequivocal success. It was. Chicago became the center of the nation's railroad industry. Now, nearly a quarter of century after Ogden helped create this mecca along the lakefront, it was devastated by fire.

Fortunately, the former mayor did not personally see it burn. He was living in New York City at the time, along with a new wife, Marian, his first. In a sad footnote to what follows, Ogden had waited until he was nearly 70 to marry. The story goes like this: In 1829, Ogden had tragically lost his childhood sweetheart, first love, and fiancée Sarah North to a sudden illness just days before they were scheduled to wed. Devastated, he kept keepsakes like pressed flowers, gloves, ribbons, some notes, and love poems that he would show to his friends and guests at the Grove. As one close associate said, Ogden remained "faithful" to Sarah by staying a bachelor until late in life. Even then, it was said his marriage to Marian was one of convenience only. When Ogden was informed Chicago was burning, he asked if anyone knew the fate of his home there. *It was spared.* That was the word he received by telegram while steaming back west by train. His beloved estate had miraculously survived the blaze. It had not. As it turned out, the dispatches were wrong: it was actually his brother Mahlon's house that was still standing. Ogden Grove, so stately just the day before, was most assuredly gone. When Ogden arrived to view the carnage firsthand, he realized everything he left behind in Chicago, including it can be assumed the precious keepsakes of his first love, Sarah, had been lost.

But that was not all. While building railroads to transport precious commodities to and from the newly established Chicago, Ogden had the foresight to invest in other ventures, including timber. Utilizing the strength of these two industries raised his capital considerably. With the help of friends, Ogden built a railway line from Chicago to Peshtigo, Wisconsin, just north of Green Bay. Peshtigo was a lush, forested area with row after row of tall pine trees and a waterway, the Peshtigo River, which effectively fed into the Bay and out into the choppy waters of Lake Michigan. Sending the logs by steamer or barge through the unpredictable

Great Lakes was risky and dangerous, so Ogden provided a safer and more proficient route by building a rail track that connected Peshtigo Harbor to Chicago.

Ogden's bad luck was palpable. Around the same time he received the awful news that Chicago was burning to the ground, another telegram arrived. This time the news was accurate—and grim. A massive firestorm had consumed Peshtigo, fueled by wind and flying embers which danced from tree to tree, creating a fast and deadly inferno. The lumberyard Ogden helped fund and establish near his rail line didn't stand a chance. In an instant it was razed, and everything, the yards, the outbuildings, the stacks upon stacks of timber ready to be shipped, were gone. Even worse, early reports indicated the loss of life would be extensive. Many families who lived and worked at Ogden's logging camps were either missing or presumed dead. The sobering facts would soon emerge. An estimated 2,200 perished in the blaze, including 1,800 or nearly all save a few hundred of the residents from the town of Peshtigo, making it the deadliest fire in U.S. history. Chicago's death toll of 300, while still tragic, pales in comparison. Yet, by virtue of being on the same day in history and because of Chicago's status as one of the world's great cities, the Great Chicago Fire became the stuff of legend; the rural Peshtigo fire, despite its staggering death toll, became an afterthought.

The backlash against Train and his incendiary words would eventually fade. There simply wasn't enough evidence to convict him or others that the fire was deliberately set by anarchists. Train, however, sensed an increase in interest in his name at least and set out to exploit it. He continued a frenzied pace of speech after speech, city after city, as he had done in the spring and summer earlier that year. Only this time, the curious as well as the furious came out to see him. "All aboard! Get aboard the express train of George Francis Train!" he shouted, as supporters danced down the aisle, bending their elbows and winding their arms clockwise in sync, like the pistons of a moving train. Although a Train associate predicted "Six Million Votes, for the Child of Fate," only Train himself and his most devoted followers seemed to think they had a chance to win the presidency in 1872. The momentum of his campaign after the Chicago Fire fiasco continued right until the point when Train defended his fellow fringe opponent Victoria Woodhull against libel and was jailed.

While the *Times* fanned the flames of suspicion about Train and the anarchist group from Paris, even more controversial and diabolical accusations surfaced as to why the city was doomed and presumably under attack. No doubt the bitterness of war was still on the mind of many hardline Southerners who saw the fire as retribution. "God adjusts balances," voiced one biased southern Indiana newspaper, making comparisons to the burning of Atlanta as an example. "Maybe with Chicago, the books are now squared."

Perhaps the reason for the fire was more spiritual than political, as many radicals across the country pointed to the sins of Chicago as reason the Almighty himself would punish the city. "They tell me you are wicked and I believe them, for I have seen your painted women under the gas lamps luring the farm boys," Carl Sandburg wrote in the most famous of his many poems about the city. The temperance movement leaders, who had already stopped or slowed the use of alcohol in many states, were especially harsh. Chicago had just permitted its saloons to be open on Sundays, they pointed out, and so God intervened. In one rather comical explanation, a fire extinguisher salesman angered by poor sales set the blaze to drum up more business. But all these tall tales needed more substantial proof. They were all quickly dismissed in the public eye, except for one.

And it has never been forgotten.

3

I could not tell

⟡ In 1938, nearly 70 years after fire ravaged the city, a new movie opened in theaters across the country. Entitled *In Old Chicago*, it tells the story of a woman named Molly O'Leary who had just moved to Chicago with her husband Patrick and three sons. When Patrick is killed after foolishly chasing after a train with a horse-drawn wagon, she suddenly finds herself alone and widowed. A laundress by trade, Molly soon opens a shop in a poor, working-class area of Chicago known as "The Patch."

Meanwhile, her three sons find big city life to their liking. Each finds a girl he wants to marry. Then one son, named Dion, starts to involve himself with a local businessman, Gil Warren, a shady character indeed. Dion becomes enamored with a pretty barroom singer named Belle and together they devise a plan to bribe local politicians to set up a saloon on the street, much to Warren's liking, who has political aspirations of his own. Eventually, Warren runs for mayor against Dion's brother Jack, and Dion must choose between business and family. Belle, who rebukes Dion for having eyes on a local senator's daughter, sides with Jack, who wants to reform "The Patch" and in effect put Dion and Warren's devious practices to rest. To keep Belle from testifying against him, Dion marries her.

Molly does not intervene but clearly considers Belle the loose cannon, not her son. Late one night, a fight breaks out between Dion and Jack over Belle's loyalty. Molly finds out about it while tending to Daisy, a dairy cow the family kept in a barn next to their home. In distress, Molly runs out of the barn without taking the kerosene lantern. When Daisy inadvertently kicks the lantern over, it ignites the hay on the barn floor.

Soon, the building, the block, and the city are in flames.

Of course, this overtly imaginative tale was all a screenwriter's version of events, mostly fiction and written for the silver screen. But in 1871, shortly after the fire, the stories that emerged about Mrs. O'Leary and her cow were nearly as sensationalized as the film that would later dramatize it.

First, the real Mrs. O'Leary was named Catherine, not Molly, and she lived on De Koven Street, in an immigrant neighborhood filled with what one reporter described as "one-story frame dwellings, cow-stables, pig-sties, corn cribs, and sheds innumerable." "The Patch" was a made-up name, although there was an area of rockeries near the O'Leary home called "Conley's Patch." The portrayal of a working-class, low-income neighborhood wasn't far off.

Catherine's husband Patrick, a Civil War veteran and laborer, was actually alive and well when the real fire started. The O'Leary's had five children; the oldest, a girl, was 14. According to those who have done the research, including Robert Cromie, the journalist who interviewed first descendants of victims and spoke to "several survivors with vivid memories of the disaster," Catherine was no laundress as she would later be portrayed in the film, but instead ran a milk route in the neighborhood. The actress who portrayed the Molly character in the movie was dowdy and matronly. According to Cromie, however, the real Catherine O'Leary was described as "a plump woman about thirty-five [years in age]."

The barn in question was part of three structures near the corner of De Koven and Taylor Streets: a "small shingled house" used as a rental, a cottage the family lived in behind the rental, and the barn behind the cottage next to the alley. The barn housed five cows, a calf, and a horse. "Added to Pat's wages and the rent from the second cottage, the income from the milk made the O'Leary's

"The Innocent Cause: or the Origin of Chicago Fire". Copelin and Hine, Chicago, IL, 1871. The Robert N. Dennis Collection of Stereoscopic Views, Miriam and Ira D. Wallach Division of Arts, Prints and Photographs, public domain.

figures of downright affluence by the standards of the neighbor-hood," Cromie writes. It is here, at the very barn, that the legend of Mrs. O'Leary and her cow begins.

But is it true?

Several neighbors claim the O'Learys were sleeping at the time the fire broke out. These included Daniel "Peg Leg" Sullivan, who visited the O'Learys shortly before they retired for the night. He later testified that the O'Learys were all at home and they were readying for bed. Since it had been only around 8:30 in the evening, Sullivan was asked why. "The old woman said she didn't feel so well," Sullivan told authorities. Another neighbor, Dennis Rogan, who also claimed to have visited the O'Leary home before the fire, says he asked Catherine directly why she was going to bed at such a time. "I have a sore foot," was her reply. Besides, Rogan recalls, she had to be up at five to milk the cows.

Next door to the O'Learys and living in the rental house were the McLaughlins. A party was being held in honor of a family member who had just arrived from Ireland. Fiddle music was being played and beer was served thanks to several "growlers" imported from the local saloon just a half block down the street. Sullivan, who had just left the O'Learys, home, stopped briefly and sat on a high sidewalk near a fence to listen to the merry sounds coming from the McLaughlin home.

Just as he turned around to leave, he spotted a "sudden spear of flame" coming from the side of the O'Leary barn. The barn was burning quickly, and Sullivan alerted the neighbors. "I couldn't run very quick," Sullivan said. "I could holler loud enough but could not run." Once he reached the barn, he could only find a "half burned" calf inside. Meanwhile, the flying embers had reached another barn near the O'Leary home. The O'Learys, including the children, were roused from sleep by Sullivan's cries of, "FIRE! FIRE! FIRE!"

This is the version as told by both Sullivan and Rogan during an inquiry held to determine how the fire, which originated on De Koven Street, began. By that time, there were newspaper articles suggesting that Mrs. O'Leary was indeed the unsuspecting cul-prit. According to reports, Mrs. O'Leary apparently went to the barn shortly before the fire to milk one of the cows. She left the lamp, and the cow tipped it over. When Mrs. O'Leary was called to testify, however, she insisted she did not milk her cows at night. Instead, she reiterated, she was in bed as others had vouched. She was asked if anyone other than herself could have been in the barn that night. The curious question was followed by an even more curious answer. "Yes, sir. I have heard of it. I have heard from other folks," was her reply.

Mrs. O'Leary explained that a neighbor named Mrs. White told her that some of the attendees of the McLaughlins' party were in the barn that night milking the cows for their own benefit. "Had these persons in your house been in the habit of getting milk there before if they wanted it?" she was asked. "No, sir," was her response. Investigators must not have known about this surprising revelation before asking. The inquiry took place at the end of November 1871, more than a month after the blaze. Rumors of Mrs. O'Leary, the lantern, and the cow had already been circulating. In many minds, the mystery was solved. Under oath, however, Catherine O'Leary refuted the claims and answered directly the question, "Do you know how the fire was caught?" with a resounding, "I could not tell."

Regardless of who saw what where, the tale of Mrs. O'Leary's cow starting the fire has survived the test of time. However, according to contemporary scholars of Chicago history, the O'Learys' story was not central to local and national newspaper coverage after the fire. Moreover, the reports that did appear were factually misleading. The *Chicago Herald,* for example, mentioning the barn, called Mrs. O'Leary "a woman named Scully." While the *Times,* much more biting, claimed she was an "Irish hag, age of 70."

Logically, the story seemed to contain more myth than fact, and several keen observers noted such. The editors of the *Chicago Tribune,* for example, just didn't buy it. "The story of the attempt to milk a cow by the light of a kerosene lamp, and the rapid-firing of the cowshed, is known to be untrue," they wrote in a treatise released shortly after the blaze. Another quickly released book written by Frank Luzerne and titled *The Lost City!* also disputes the tale: "The story about an old woman who went into her shed to milk a cow by the light of a kerosene lamp, which lamp said cow kicked over, is pure fabrication." Luzerne then points out a plausible alternative. "The *Journal of Commerce,*" he notes, "remarks that in high wind smokers might stop there [meaning O'Leary's barn] for the purpose of striking a match [more] than any other part of the neighborhood. A spark alighted on this tinder of hay and shingles, and fanned by the wind, would soon wrap the slight barn in flames." This would prove to be a more reasonable theory and one that eventually exonerated poor Mrs. O'Leary. In fact, it was first observer, Daniel "Peg Leg" Sullivan, who most likely tried to cover up his own actions that night, devious or not.

In 1911, 40 years after the fact, a former reporter for the *Chicago Republican* named Michael Ahern claimed it was he and a fellow reporter named Jim Haynie of the *Chicago Times* who concocted the story of the cow kicking over the lamp after finding a broken kerosene lamp in the barn's rubble. While it made sense, especially given the wild exploits of print journalism then, Ahern's story has holes. The tale of the cow and lantern first appeared in the *Evening Journal,* a rival newspaper, the day after the fire. Therefore, if it did appear in the *Times* as Ahern suggested, it was copied. Also, why did Ahern wait so long to tell his side of story? After Ahern's death in 1927, another reporter named John Kelley wrote a letter disclosing Ahern's long-held belief that it was an unidentified pipe smoker behind the shed that caused the hay to ignite, not the lantern, the cow, or Mrs. O'Leary's negligence. Nevertheless, even if the story was made up as Kelley suggested, the impact was long-lasting.

The truth about why the fire occurred could be found in an inquiry report put out by the police and fire department. The report puts the blame squarely on the city for shoddy construction and lax building code inspections. It also criticizes the lack of funding for more fire apparatus, which they claim, with the availability of more fireboats at the ready, could have contained the fire on the West Side of the city before it spread. The cow was irrelevant. Accidents happen and fires occur, especially during long, hot, dry spells. The city, while known for a productive fire department, lacked the manpower and resources to handle one of this magnitude.

While the report's findings were straightforward and honest, the inquiring public wanted more. They wanted a good story and for a time the incendiary words of George Francis Train and the actions of Mrs. O'Leary and her cow were all the rage. Train, for his part, got a pass, but Mrs. O' Leary wasn't so lucky. She lived a hermit's life of exclusion after the fire, choosing to hide from publicity rather than profit from it.

To avoid the scrutiny, the O'Leary family moved several times after the fire. Catherine reportedly left her home only to run errands and go to church on Sundays. Her refusal to be interviewed only meant that reporters made things up. Though she never allowed herself to be photographed, fakes appeared. So did drawings, most depicting an old, angry woman, and even one that made her look like she was possessed by the devil.

By the time of her death in 1895, the woman who remained the symbolic figurehead of the Great Chicago Fire was mostly left alone, except for one time a year. Every October, around the anniversary of the fire, the press would come knocking on Mrs. O'Leary's door, hoping she would change her mind and tell her side of the story again. Perhaps, they thought, she might want to change fate by refuting the theories again and rebuking those who chose to defame her name.

She never did.

4
I have some
terrible news

⟨✍⟩ Train, on the other hand, was emboldened by the press he received. In fact, his popularity seemed to rise after the fire debacle. Although his run for the presidency was more a curiosity, his jailing just before the election seemed to establish that he was not of sound mind. Immediately after being released from New York's Tombs, as Train put it, "I went down town, had a bath, got a good meal, put on better clothes, and bought a passage for England."

Train would return to America, make a few public appearances, including the "electrifying" turn at the Chicago's World Fair, and then disappear from sight. He spent the final years of life in a New York hotel room, mostly penniless and alone. His last noteworthy accomplishment was his third and final trip around the world in 1892. "I eclipsed all previous records," he wrote. "To these trips I attach no more importance, I hope, than is fairly their due. But they were, as I consider them, merely incidents in a life that has better things to show."

Two years before his death in 1904, at the age of 74, Train released his autobiography: *My Life in Many States and in Foreign Lands*. Train was ailing and dictated his words to a writer. "If I should fail at any point," he said, "this will be due to some wavering of memory, and not to intention."

One bitter memory was jogged shortly before he began work on the book. Train's aunt Abigail, now in her 90s, sent George a letter she had only recently found. It was from Train's father the day he sent young George on a steamship to live with the grandmother and his two aunts, Abigail and Alice. In the letter, Oliver Train writes about the bitterness and guilt he felt of parting with "my lovely boy." He envisioned a better life for his son after the sudden death of his wife and daughters from the yellow fever epidemic. "I part with George as if I was parting with my right eye," he writes mournfully. "But 'tis for his good and the happiness of all that he go... [for] he is no ordinary boy, but is destined for a great scholar."

George never saw his father again, and the letter was lost for decades until Abigail discovered it tucked away in the attic of her old farmhouse. The rest of the story, then, explains the reason why it was missing for so long. In 1840, seven years after apparently putting the letter away for safe keeping, Alice Train Winslow was a victim of a steamboat wreck on a cold January night in the Long Island Sound. Ten years old at the time, George was in school during a blinding snowstorm when suddenly there was knocking at the schoolhouse door. It was George's Uncle Emery. The teacher called for George. "Your uncle has just arrived," she said, "and he wants to take you home with him." Emery had come from Boston by sleigh. He was headed to his mother's house to tell the others. George found out first. "I have some terrible news," Emery told the boy. "The *Lexington* was wrecked and burned. Your aunt was lost."

Alice was not traveling alone. Harrison Winslow, her husband, had recently passed, and she was accompanying his body to Boston for burial in the family plot. Her father-in-law William and Harrison's brother John were also on board the *Lexington*. Now they were all gone.

Train would never forget the day, and in campaign speeches, referenced a story about the ship's bell which he was told remained intact, floated away from the wreckage, and lodged in some rocks along the shoreline. As only Train could do, he compared the bell to a stalled political ideology, one which obviously discouraged him.

"It was like the bell of the *Lexington*," he said, "caught upon the rocks, clanging dolorously in every wind, and tolling perpetually for the dead."

George Francis Train shortly before his death. The Library of Congress
[January 28, 1904].

ᴄᴚᴏ George Francis Train found success, even fame. Still, he always seemed to find a way to diminish his own worth, either by actions, words, or—as some claim—just plain lunacy. Only after a long exile, and fearing his stories would be lost to time, did he document all his accomplishments. "It does not so much matter, what I may have thought of myself or what I now think of myself," he transcribed. "What does matter is what I may have done. I stand on my achievement."

With that in mind, it is often said that history is remembered only because it was documented and saved. The rest is lost forever. The lives you just experienced were never lost. They were recorded once and left for generations to rediscover. Whether time diminished that memory doesn't matter. The purpose of the story was determined long ago when it grabbed someone's attention, challenged someone's soul, and ultimately moved someone enough to write it down or at least to remember it until someone else did. As essayist Jill Lepore wrote, "Behold the historian. His hand holds the pen. His eye lingers on the past."

Acknowledgments

Since this is a book based on quite a few sources, I'm indebted to the many authors and librarians who provided materials. I'm especially grateful to those who answered my calls and emails when questions or concerns went beyond the click of a button. A special thanks goes to the staff at my local library branch in Morton, Illinois, who gladly helped me find and obtain a plethora of materials.

A very special recognition goes to the team at Amika Press, particularly Sarah Koz, John Manos and Dr. Jay Amberg. They have supported and encouraged me since Amika Press published my first book in 2012. Today, I'm proud to be a part of growing group of terrific authors with books in all genres.

My appreciation goes to the editor of this book, Mark Larson, whom I met when Mark inquired about making a Readers' Theater interpretation of *The Wreck of the Columbia*. Mark knows my writing well and made this book better through his suggestions, steady guidance, and expert copy editing. Thanks also goes to Amy Sawyer for her precise proofreading.

Others who contributed directly and indirectly to this book through their friendship and encouragement include (in no particular order): Mike Zurski, Randy Whalen, Greg Batton, Christoph Traugott, Mike Wild of Alpha Media, Norman V. Kelly, my blog and online followers, and my extended family—in-laws, cousins, and niece Cheyenne.

Finally, I offer infinite thanks to my immediate family. First to my children, Sam and Nora, who through their inquiries and curiosity have had a large influence on my work. And most deeply, to my wife Connie, who is my rock and the foundation of our home. Her unwavering support is the reason why I'm able to do all that I do.

Bibliography

In lieu of citations, I have embedded as much information about source materials as possible within the text. In cases in which no single direct origin can be attributed, the material is marked as originating in the source from which it was found.

Alcock, John; Brown, Arthur Whitten. *Our Transatlantic Flight*. William Kimber, 1969

Anthony, Katharine. *Susan B. Anthony: Her Personal History and Her Era*. New York: Doubleday & Co., Inc., 1954

Bales, Richard F. *The Great Chicago Fire and the Myth of Mrs. O'Leary's Cow*. North Carolina: McFarland & Company, Inc., 2002

Bennie, Paul. *The Great Chicago Fire of 1871*. New York: Chelsea House, 2008

Berg, A. Scott. *Lindbergh*. New York: G.P. Putnam's Sons, 1998

Berton, Pierre. *Niagara: A History of the Falls*. New York: Kodansha America, 1997

Brands, H.W. *American Colossus: The Triumph of Capitalism*. New York: Doubleday, 2010

Connell, Evan S. *Son of the Morning Star: Custer and the Little Bighorn*. New York: Farrar, Straus and Giroux, 1984

Crouse, Russell. *Mr. Currier and Mr. Ives: A Note on Their Lives and Times*. New York: Garden City Publishing, 1930

Cussler, Clive. *The Sea Hunters: True Adventures with Famous Shipwrecks*. New York: Simon & Schuster, 1996

Davenport-Hines, Richard. *Voyagers of the Titanic*. New York: Harper-Collins, 2012

Dickens, Charles. *American Notes: For General Circulation*. London: Chapman & Hall, 1842

Dolnick, Edward. *Down the Great Unknown: John Wesley Powell's 1869 Journey of Discovery and Tragedy through the Grand Canyon*. New York: HarperCollins, 2001

Foster, Allen. *Around the World with Citizen Train: The Sensational Adventures of the Real Phileas Fogg*. Dublin, Ireland: Merlin Publishing, 2002

Fox, Stephen. *The Ocean Railway: Isambard Kingdom Brunel, Samuel Cunard and the Revolutionary World of the Great Atlantic Steamships.* London: HarperCollins Publishers, 2003

Garvey, Timothy. *Public Sculptor: Lorado Taft and the Beautification of Chicago.* Chicago: University of Illinois Press, 1988

Gess, Denise; Lutz, William. *Firestorm at Peshtigo: A Town, Its People, and the Deadliest Fire in American History.* New York: Henry Holt and Company, 2002

Goldsmith, Barbara. *Other Powers: The Age of Suffrage, Spiritualism, and the Scandalous Victoria Woodhull.* New York: Alfred A. Knopf, 1998

Goldstone, Lawrence. *Birdmen: The Wright Brothers, Glenn Curtiss, and the Battle to Control the Skies.* New York: Ballantine Books, 2014

Goodman, Matthew. *Eighty Days: Nellie Bly and Elizabeth Bisland's History-Making Race Around the World.* New York: Ballantine Books, 2013

Holmes, Richard. *Falling Upwards: How We Took to the Air.* New York: First Vintage Books, 2014

Jackson, Joe. *Atlantic Fever: Lindbergh, His Competitors, and the Race to Cross the Atlantic.* New York: Farrar, Straus and Giroux, 2012

Jessen, Gene. *Powder Puff Derby of 1929: The True Story of the First Women's Cross-Country Air Race.* Illinois: Sourcebooks, Inc., 2002

Jordan, Humfrey. *Mauretania: Landfalls and Departures of Twenty-Five Years.* London: Hodder & Stoughton Limited, 1936

Jules-Verne, Jean. *Jules Verne: A Biography.* New York: Taplinger Publishing Company, 1976

Kilgallen, Dorothy. *Girl Around the World.* Philadelphia: David McKay Co., 1936

Kroeger, Brooke. *Nellie Bly: Daredevil, Reporter, Feminist.* New York: Times Books, 1994

Larson, Erik. *The Devil in the White City: Murder, Magic, and Madness at the Fair That Changed America.* New York: Vintage Books, 2003

Lebow, Eileen E. *Cal Rodgers and the Vin Fiz: The First Transcontinental Flight.* Washington D.C.: Smithsonian Institution, 1989

Lepore, Jill. *Book of Ages: The Life and Opinions of Jane Franklin.* New York: Alfred A. Knopf, 2013

MacPherson, Myra. *The Scarlet Sisters: Sex, Suffrage, and Scandal in the Gilded Age.* New York: Hachette Book Group, 2014

McCullough, David. *The Wright Brothers.* Simon & Schuster, 2015

Miller, Donald L. *City of the Century: The Epic of Chicago and the Making of America.* New York: Simon & Schuster, 1996

Murray, Joan. *Queen of the Mist: The Forgotten Heroine of Niagara.* Boston: Beacon Press, 1999

Pacyga, Dominic A. *Chicago: A Biography.* Chicago: The University of Chicago Press, 2009

Peters, Harry T. *Currier & Ives: Printmakers to the American People.* New York: Doubleday, Doran & Co., Inc., 1942

Rolt, L.T.C. *Isambard Kingdom Brunel: Engineer, Visionary and Magnetic Personality, He Transformed the Face of England.* London & New York: Penguin Books, 1957

Schlereth, Thomas J. *Victorian America: Transformations in Everyday Life 1876-1915*. New York: HarperCollins, 1991

Scudder, Janet. *Modeling My Life*. New York: Harcourt Brace & Co., 1925

Stein, E.P. *Flight of the Vin Fiz: Being an Account of the Wondrous Adventures of Calbraith P. Rodgers and his Flying Machine in the Grand Coast-to-Coast $50,000 Air Race*. New York: Arbor House, 1985

Stashower, Daniel. *The Beautiful Cigar Girl: Mary Rogers, Edgar Allan Poe, and the Invention of Murder*. New York: Dutton, 2006

Strausbaugh, John. *City of Sedition: The History of New York During the Civil War*. New York: Hachette Book Group, 2016

Stiles, T.J. *The First Tycoon: The Epic Life of Cornelius Vanderbilt*. New York: Vintage Books, 2010

Stimson, A.L. *History of the Express Business: Including the Origin of the Railway System in America, and the Relation of Both to the Increase of New Settlements and the Prosperity of Cities in the United States*. New York: Baker, Godwin & Co. Printers, 1881

Stoutemeyer, Helen Louise. *Sands of Time: 150 Years Around Chatsworth, Illinois*. Illinois: HLPS Publishing, 1991

Stoutemeyer, Helen Louise. *The Train That Never Arrived: A Saga of the Niagara Excursion Train that Wrecked Between Chatsworth and Piper City, August 10, 1887*. Illinois: Cornbelt Press, 1980

Taylor, Annie Edson. *Over The Falls: Annie Edson Taylor's Story of Her Trip; How the Horseshoe Fall Was Conquered*. London: Forgotten Books, 2017

Tobin, James. *To Conquer The Air: The Wright Brothers and the Great Race for Flight*. New York: Free Press, 2003

Train, George Francis. *My Life in Many States and in Foreign Lands*. New York: D. Appleton & Co., 1902

Underhill, Lois Beachy. *The Woman Who Ran for President: The Many Lives of Victoria Woodhull*. New York: Bridge Works Publishing, 1995

Weller, Allen Stuart. *Lorado Taft: The Chicago Years*. Chicago: University of Illinois Press, 2014

Winchester, Simon. *The Men Who United the States: America's Explorers, Inventors, Eccentrics, and Mavericks, and the Creation of One Nation, Indivisible*. New York: Harper Perennial, 2013

Zacks, Richard. *Island of Vice: Theodore Roosevelt's Quest to Clean Up Sin-Loving New York*. New York: Doubleday, 2012

Index

Serrell, Edward, 62
Shaum, John H., Jr., 169
shipbuilding, 8, 161, 162, 165
shipwreck, 21-24, 169
silver, 3, 19, 21, 22, 24, 108
Simonson, Charles, 8
Sirius (steamship), 162, 164
Smithsonian Institute, 156
Stanton, Elizabeth Cady, 203
states' rights, 201
steamboat
    and Brunel, 161, 162, 164, 165
    and Collins, 167
    and Cunard, 165-167, 169, 170
    and Dickens, 167
    and *Lexington,* 3-8, 10-13
    and *Mauretania,* 168-170
    and *Titanic,* 169, 170
    versus railroad, 7
Steamboat Transportation Company, 6, 11
Stiles, T.J., 6, 64, 200
Stimson, T.J., 24, 25
Stone, E.J., 25
Stonington Rail Line, 10, 11
Stoutemyer, Louise, 107
suicide, 87
Sullivan, Daniel "Peg Leg", 221, 223
suspension bridge, 61, 62, 68, 69
Sybil's Cave, 43, 44

T

Table Rock, 81-83
Taft, Lorado, 54, 55, 57
Tait, Arthur Fitzwilliam, 50
Tammany Hall, 52
Tarbell, Ida M., 135, 136
Taylor, Annie Edson, 86-90, 92, 95-102, 104
Tiffany, Louis Comfort, 54
Tilton, Theodore, 205
Titanic (ship), 170
Toledo, Peoria & Western (train), 76
Tracey, William, 25
Train, Enoch, 128, 129
Train, George Francis, 70, 71, 118, 119, 125, 126

and Anthony, 206
and Bly, 139, 140
and *Lexington* disaster, 226
final years of, 225
and Great Chicago Fire, 198, 210-212, 214, 216, 217
photograph of, 127, 227
and presidential bid, 207, 216, 217
and shipping business, 128
and travel around the world, 129, 130, 142, 144, 225
and Woodhull and Claflin, 192, 206-208
at World's Columbian Exposition, 192, 193
Trans-Atlantic Balloon Corporation, 111
Transcontinental Railroad, 65
Truesdale, Fred, 95
Tweed, Boss, 52

U

United States, Constitution of the, 201, 202
United States Literary Gazette, 33
United States Mail Steamship Company, 167

V

Van Buren, Martin, 46, 47
Vanderbilt, Cornelius
    and *Citizen,* 12
    and *Lexington,* 6-8
    and Niagara River Bridge Company, 60-62, 64
    photograph of, 9
    in train accident, 14
    and Woodhull and Claflin, 199-201
Vanderbilt, Jacob, 11, 12, 15
Verne, Jules, 129, 130, 138, 142, 145, 146
Vickers Vimy, 171, 181
Victoria, Queen, 160
Vin Fiz Flyer, 177, 179, 180
Virginian-Pilot, 151
voting rights, 201, 202, 206

About the Author

Ken Zurski is a longtime broadcaster, author and speaker based out of Peoria, Illinois. A native of the Chicagoland area and a veteran of radio news, Ken released his first book, *The Wreck of the Columbia*, in 2012. *Unremembered* is his third book. Ken resides in Morton, Illinois with his wife, Connie, and two children, Sam and Nora.

Visit his website at unrememberedhistory.com, follow him on Facebook at @kenzurskiauthor or @unrememberedhistory, and find him on Twitter at @kzurski.

Made in the USA
Lexington, KY
21 September 2018